Improving the Composability of Department of Defense Models and Simulations

Paul K. Davis, Robert H. Anderson

Prepared for the Defense Modeling and Simulation Office
Approved for public release, distribution unlimited

RAND
NATIONAL DEFENSE RESEARCH INSTITUTE

The research described in this report was sponsored by the Defense Modeling and Simulation Office (DMSO). The research was conducted in RAND's National Defense Research Institute, a federally funded research and development center supported by the Office of the Secretary of Defense (OSD), the Joint Staff, the unified commands, and the defense agencies under Contract DASW01-01-C-0004.

Library of Congress Cataloging-in-Publication Data

Davis, Paul K., 1943–
Improving the composability of Department of Defense models and simulations / Paul K. Davis, Robert A. Anderson.
p. cm.
Includes bibliographical references.
"MG-101."
ISBN 0-8330-3525-8 (pbk. : alk. paper)
1. Military art and science—United States—Mathematical models. 2. Military art and science—United States—Simulation methods. 3. Operations research. 4. Military research—United States. 5. Military planning—United States. I. Anderson, Robert H., 1959– II.Title.

U104.D3823 2004
355'.001'1—dc22

2003026513

The RAND Corporation is a nonprofit research organization providing objective analysis and effective solutions that address the challenges facing the public and private sectors around the world. RAND's publications do not necessarily reflect the opinions of its research clients and sponsors.

Cover design by Maritta Tapanainen

Published 2003 by the RAND Corporation
1700 Main Street, P.O. Box 2138, Santa Monica, CA 90407-2138
1200 South Hayes Street, Arlington, VA 22202-5050
201 North Craig Street, Suite 202, Pittsburgh, PA 15213-1516
RAND URL: http://www.rand.org/
To order RAND documents or to obtain additional information, contact
Distribution Services: Telephone: (310) 451-7002;
Fax: (310) 451-6915; Email: order@rand.org

Preface

This monograph is concerned with improving the composability of future models and simulations developed or used by the Department of Defense. It was prepared in response to a request by the Defense Modeling and Simulation Office (DMSO) to provide independent advice to assist in developing a program to pursue composability issues. The monograph presents many suggestions on both policies and investments that would enhance prospects for composability. It is intended primarily for officials and other individuals familiar with basic concepts and issues of modeling, simulation, and composability, but definitions and examples are included that make the study reasonably accessible to other interested consumers of modeling and simulation.

This research was conducted for DMSO within the Acquisition and Technology Policy Center of the RAND Corporation's National Defense Research Institute, a federally funded research and development center sponsored by the Office of the Secretary of Defense, the Joint Staff, the unified commands, and the defense agencies.

Comments are welcome and should be addressed to the authors at RAND's Santa Monica, CA, office:

Paul_Davis@rand.org Robert_Anderson@rand.org

Contents

Figures

Tables

Summary

In modeling and simulation (M&S), composability is the capability to select and assemble components in various combinations to satisfy specific user requirements meaningfully. It has sometimes been seen as the elusive holy grail of modeling and simulation; past Department of Defense (DoD) efforts to achieve it have had distinctly mixed success despite the many technological developments that have occurred over the past 5 to 10 years. In reviewing this situation, we have sought to identify key elements for defining a path to future success.

Diagnosis

There are many reasons for seeking composability when dealing with complex systems, but the basic question addressed here is, What are the factors that determine what can be "composed" when, and with how much expense and risk?

In the aggregate, those factors include

- The complexity of the system being modeled.
- The difficulty of the objective for the context in which the composite M&S will be used.
- The strength of underlying science and technology, including standards.

- Human considerations, such as the quality of management, having a common community of interest, and the skill and knowledge of the work force.

Figure S.1 shows a richer breakdown of these factors. Unfortunately, there is no single Gordian knot—many factors currently limit success.

Notionally, if these factors could be roughly quantified, they could be used to characterize the probability of success of a particular proposed composition effort. A parametric plot of risk might look something like Figure S.2, which is purely speculative but qualitatively reasonable. Risk rises with some measure of "effective" size and complexity, but it rises faster if the composite M&S will be used in rigorous work (i.e., work requiring that well-controlled and reproducible results be used for matters of choice), and it rises extremely fast if any of several danger factors are present. These include poor management; the crossing of many military or cultural boundaries in attempting the composition; and a poor understanding of what is being modeled, worsened by a weak treatment of uncertainty. In these cases, the risk of failure is high even if expenditures are increased; these shortcomings cannot be overcome by simply throwing money at the problem.

With this image in mind for assessing risk as a function of factors, we consider all of the factors in Figure S.1. Doing so increases humility, which has sometimes been notably absent in the thinking of composability advocates. Customers—those who pay for and hope to use the fruits of composability-driven efforts for practical purposes such as weapon acquisition, training, or warfighting—need realistic expectations and assistance in establishing those expectations and related requirements. **The appealing imagery of arbitrary plug-and-play is fatally flawed for complex models,** even with adherence to the standards of DoD's high-level architecture. The viewgraph-level metaphor of jigsaw-puzzle pieces snapping together is not appropriate either, except, for example, when the components have been carefully designed with the intention of fitting together neatly in a known

Figure S.1
Factors Affecting the Difficulty of M&S Composition

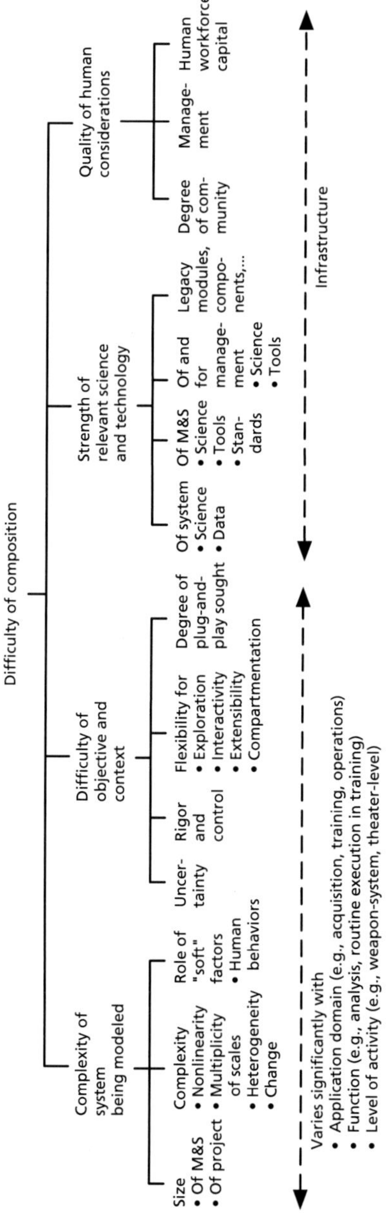

RAND *MG101-S.1*

Figure S.2
Notional Curve of Risk Versus Attributes of the Composite M&S Being Attempted

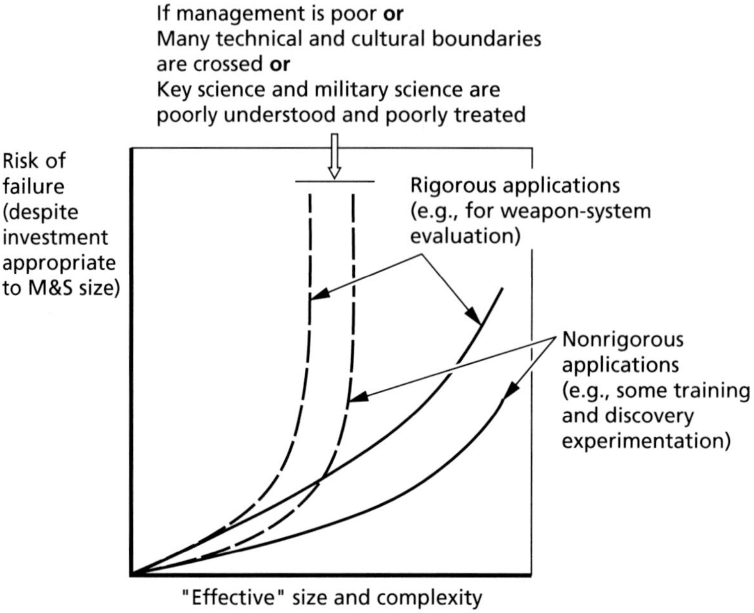

RAND *MG101-S.2*

context, or when the components happen to deal with stable, well-defined, and usually low-level matters such as a simple physics calculation. The basic reason for this is that composing models is not as simple as composing software components that provide straightforward and readily compartmented services. That is, while the engineering of pure software composition is notoriously difficult, **model composition is much more difficult, something often not appreciated even by good software engineers: Models are different.** The more-complex model components have typically been developed for particular purposes and depend on context-sensitive assumptions, some of which are tacit. When composing such component models, "successful" composition efforts often require days, weeks, or even months, most of which go into understanding and modifying would-be components and interfaces so that the resulting composed model will be reasonably valid for its intended use. This process is not likely to change drastically, i.e., to a matter of minutes to days, except for relatively simple atomic components, because so many of the problems are substantive, rather than being mere issues of syntax or superficial semantics. This said, there are important opportunities for technological progress, as in reuse of at least a significant number of components, the use of metadata for search and ranking of plausible components, and rapid evaluation in new contexts. The opportunities are quite different, depending on whether the function intended is simple or, as is the case in many exercises, fairly loose, even if complicated, or both complex and rigorous, as in some analyses. Generally, we see the opportunities for progress as being greatest for enhanced man-machine efficiency and effectiveness, not for automated model composition.

As a measure of how serious the disconnect between hype and reality has been on composability, some experts in a recent workshop, experts who understand composability issues and might be expected to favor composability per se, said candidly that they often find themselves arguing vociferously *against* composition efforts because the people proposing them do not understand how ill served end-users would be by connecting modules developed in different places and times and for different purposes, or how hard it is to understand the substantive consequences of connecting such modules. We agree with this assessment and believe that **DoD should focus its composability efforts on those domains and circumstances in which they actually make most sense—not for their own sake, but in a "business-case" sense.** A related vision for DoD is the potentially great advantage of having first-rate virtual environments for assessing alternative weapons or doctrinal concepts, environments that could be used for some years with many changes of individual modules but with most aspects of the environments being well controlled, *and* with the underlying models being open to scrutiny by all concerned so as to permit fair competition. Such a vision would have immediate implications for commercial companies, which would discover business cases for modular M&S efforts accordingly. There are parallels in simulation-based acquisition (SBA) and integrated manufacturing.

Significantly, tangible examples of composability-oriented analysis work groups have existed for some years, as illustrated in the text of this monograph with examples from the RAND Corporation and Lockheed-Martin (Sunnyvale).

Synthesis and Prescription

Given a diagnosis of the issues, what can be done to improve the situation? Here, a "systems approach" is needed, because there is no single stumbling block, but rather a set of them. There are many ways to characterize systems, but we chose to focus on "targets," that is, on objective system elements for which we can see specific measures to be taken. We suggest the following targets for a broad approach, as indicated in Figure S.3:

- *Science* (of the subjects being modeled and of the M&S activities themselves).
- *Technology, including standards* for composability.
- *Understanding* (e.g., of pitfalls, best practices, relevant metrics, and of what can reasonably be achieved).
- *Quality of management* in substantial composability efforts (including goal setting, team building, metrics setting, and collaborative methods).
- *Quality of the workforce* (e.g., education, talent, experience).
- *Health and vitality of the communitywide M&S environment*, including a motivated industrial base with a mix of stable centers of excellence and more-dynamic competition, and with sensible motivations for industrial cooperation among players in particular subject areas (e.g., developers of a major next-generation suite of weapons and doctrine, such as the Army's Future Combat System or its successor).

Our conclusions on how to achieve these are outlined below.

Figure S.3
A System View of Suggested Targets

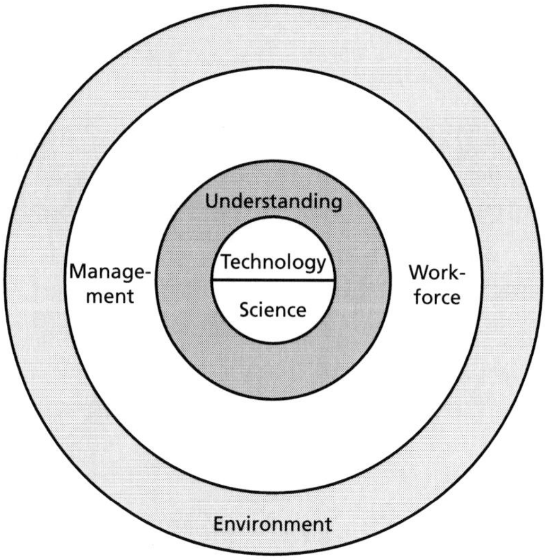

RAND *MG101-S.3-A*

Science and Technology, Including Standards

Military Science and Technology

In many instances, deep knowledge of the phenomena being modeled limits what can be accomplished. This is not a "software problem," but rather something demanding in-depth inquiry about the science of appropriate subject areas—military science, in the case of DoD models. Although DoD pursues many subjects in various studies and experiments, it typically does so unsystematically and leaves behind no settled understanding of those subjects. **DoD should instead mount military-science programs to assure a strong base of knowledge in key domains.** The Defense Modeling and Simulation Office (DMSO) should advocate for and cooperate with such programs where they exist. The efforts of DoD's Command and Control Research Program (CCRP) might be seen here as an exemplar in some respects: It has pulled together a community of people who have scientific conferences, publish thoughtful papers and books, and even generate suggested best-practices guides. Some examples of subject areas for study include effects-based operations, network-centric operations, and jointness at the tactical level (others are given in the main text). The study of each would benefit greatly from an increased ratio of science to art.

In this connection, we believe that the M&S and command, control, communications, computers, intelligence, surveillance, and reconnaissance (C4ISR) worlds need to be pursuing some fundamental issues together, because their efforts should logically supplement each other. Although the scope of M&S is much broader than that of C4ISR, pursuing this suggestion where it makes sense would have major implications for everything from system modeling (e.g., identifying and naming the entities) to the adoption of standards. The NATO C4ISR community is moving toward commercial standards.

Science and Technology of M&S

The science of modeling and simulation is substantial and growing. It involves, for example, understanding languages and notations—e.g., unified modeling language (UML) and discrete-event system specification (DEVS)—for expressing models, alternative ways to structure them—e.g., agent-based and object-oriented methods—and interoperability frameworks, such as the high-level architecture (HLA). **DoD should encourage and support M&S education and training programs that reflect this science well.**

Success in composability also depends critically on science-and-engineering advances in a number of methodologies, notably:

- *Model abstraction* and the related issues of aggregation and disaggregation. These relate to the problem of "vertical integration" and cannot be solved without working the substantive problems of the subject area. Understanding how to achieve acceptable degrees of context-specific consistency or even integration across levels is a problem of methodological theory. A key element in progress is multiresolution, multiperspective families of models and games. It should be possible to extend and translate recent advances into practical guidelines.

- *Validation.* Methods and tools are needed to facilitate assessing whether a given composition would make sense in the envisioned context. For example, how do the components' features interact? And how do risks, uncertainties, and errors propagate as components are combined? There are opportunities for near-term successes here in theory, technology, and practice.
- *Heterogeneous M&S.* Methods and tools are needed to facilitate using components described in very different representations, formalisms, and styles, including those for both discrete and continuous systems.
- *Communication: documentation and new methods of transferring models.* Better documentation is needed, as discussed below. However, new methods and tools are also needed for communicating and transferring key concepts and other essentials of components and systems. The new methods should recognize that people, even "analytical people," typically learn well by doing, e.g., when learning new commercial games, participating in war games, or being appropriately tutored.
- *Explanation mechanisms.* Whether built-in or retrofitted, explanation mechanisms, including those for agent-based models, are badly needed. Ways to express "requirements" meaningfully are also needed.
- *Intimate man-machine interactions.* These interactions and the tools facilitating them are needed at most stages of development and application.

In the text of this monograph, we suggest tentatively related initiatives for investment and management.

Standards

Protocols. Standards should be an outgrowth of progress in science and technology and an enabler of efforts. Much success has been achieved with DoD's high-level architecture (HLA) and related instruments such as the run-time infrastructure (RTI) and development tools. It appears to us, however, that a critical point has been reached on protocol-oriented standards, one at which the existing set of standards should be substantially extended or even replaced. **The time is ripe for DoD to revisit the standards, much as it did in the pre-HLA days of 1994.** There have been many successes in the years since then, but it is now time to review, revise, exploit commercial momentum, and fill in where necessary.

Fierce disagreements exist on the matter of next-generation DoD standards, even after one discounts for "theology" and enthusiasm. The language of the debate revolves, for example, around the degree to which a next-generation set of DoD standards should incorporate or be replaced by the de facto standards emerging in the broader marketplace, including model-driven architecture (MDA), extensible markup language (XML), unified modeling language (UML), and common object request broker architecture (CORBA). As for the successor to today's high-level architecture (HLA) and run-time infrastructure (RTI), there is clear need for various functional extensions, such as allowing for dynamic composability within simulations and tighter specification of models related to time management, but we believe that **DoD should hurry to realign its direction better with that of the commercial marketplace, rather than merely patching the HLA/RTI on the margin.** The principles of the HLA will probably stand up well, but the current implementation will not, because commercial developments such as web services are often faster, better, and in more rapid development. In creating an improved approach, DoD needs to deemphasize rigid adherence to detailed implementation standards, which has been a problem (as in developments that were part of the Millennium Challenge 2002 experiment). Engineers with a real and tangible product to deliver should be permitted to use what is sensible in their context. In particular, some analysis applications require precise management and control of simulation events over time, while others, such as training applications, can often be very forgiving in that respect but are quite demanding in terms of scale and the ability to combine components not designed specifically for composability. Given the diversity of applications, different implementation methods are necessary.

Model Representation, Specification, and Documentation. We also concluded that **the time is also ripe for convergence on a re-**

lated matter: higher-level representations that would simplify characterization of components, communication among individuals and groups about components and possible compositions, and evaluation of alternatives. Although there will be no permanently "right" representation, and although we do not wish to prejudge the results of a review, we note that much of the relevant community is adopting evolving features of UML, XML, and variants. These, however, are not yet sufficient, even where object orientation is appropriate. For many purposes, particularly when one is concerned about the *substantive* aspects of a composed simulation, rather than just whether it will "run," more-detailed specifications are needed in a systems framework. Some of these relate to component-level behaviors and internal logic, to sound and comprehensible ways of dealing with hierarchical coupling of modules, and to anticipation of event sequences so that time management can be specified. Another fundamental need here is to build into agreed methods of representation the requirement that the model, execution engine (simulator), and context of use (sometimes called "experimental frame") be distinguished and specified separately. Often, the validity of compositions simply cannot be assessed without such a framework. In short, supporting mechanisms are needed for evaluating the "goodness of fit" when items are composed. We believe that a community consensus on methods for accomplishing these goals could now be achieved.

Documentation would be greatly facilitated by these developments. We also suspect that **retrodocumentation would prove very worthwhile in some projects,** since legacy simulations will be with us for many years, and it is currently very difficult to know the implications of using such components as part of a larger system. Retrodocumentation has seldom been proposed in the past, because it could be very expensive if done in the detail needed for full specification. What is needed most is higher-level documentation (at a "meta" level), rather than the extremely burdensome documentation of line-by-line programs. There is as yet no agreement on precisely what such higher-level documentation would look like, but we believe—based on the considerable experience of workers in the field in actually composing systems—that much consensus could be reached on what is most valuable. This would probably be a higher-level or perhaps simplified version of the documentation described above.

Data Issues. Although not discussed in detail in this monograph, another crucial subject is data. As noted briefly in the text and in an appendix, there is already much discussion about ways to standardize data, including metadata, and ways to increase its accessibility, sharing, and reuse.

Understanding

Given the experiences of the last decade, both successful and unsuccessful, it should now be feasible to develop primers and best-practices descriptions that would greatly assist clients and developers in understanding both particular needs and what can be accomplished as a function of ambitiousness and cost, and with varying degrees of risk. This understanding seems currently to be absent in the community, perhaps a reflection of earlier naïveté. As an example, managers or agencies may demand plug-and-play because it sounds attractive, when they should instead be asking for adaptiveness (via mechanisms such as wrappers, perhaps) that would allow compositions to be achieved in minutes, days, or weeks, depending on their real needs, the need for new components, and their willingness to pay. **We suggest that DoD invest in research to turn the speculative and qualitative ideas about composability risk suggested in Figure S.2 into something more solid and empirically grounded.**

Obviously, the discussion above about next steps on standards is closely related to the ability to "understand" the state of the art of model specification and the specification of simulation experiments.

As one tangible recommendation related to management, **we urge DoD to commission independent and objective lessons-learned studies on past composability-related efforts,** such as those of JSIMS (joint simulation system), JWARS (joint warfare system), and OneSAF (entity-level battalion and below constructive simulation with semi-automated forces). It is ironic that major lessons-learned studies have been or are being conducted by the services and the joint staff on warfighting, but DoD has done nothing comparable to learn from its previous modeling and simulation composability efforts. Prompt action is needed because the information will be lost as people retire and existing records disappear.

Management

Even with the best science, technology, and concept, composing large M&S systems can be doomed to failure by inadequate management. **A systematic effort is needed to define requirements and methods for developing first-rate managers, educated at the appropriate time in their careers about the special needs of complex M&S projects.** This must include acquainting managers with the special problems of *model* composition. The suggested recommendations address actions relating to credentialing, at-the-time education, primers, partnerships, and changes of military rotation cycles. The content of primers for managers would include realistic goal setting, assessing talent and team building, collaborative-management tools, and establishment of sensible metrics that do not have perverse side effects.

Many of the measures needed here are much more general than those of concern to DMSO. Preparing people for systems engineering, for example, is a broad challenge. However, if DMSO wishes composability efforts to be successful, it cannot merely assume that "someone else" will take care of these issues. It should team with other government and industry groups, such as the Defense Systems Management College, to promote appropriate initiatives.

One aspect of management is that of having the right tools. As discussed under environment (below), we would envision centralized configuration management and virtual repositories of candidate components.

The Workforce

In the past, those building even large-scale M&S systems of systems have seldom been trained for this demanding activity. As with management, there is a need for related systematic education, selection, and training. And, as with management initiatives, much could be done while teaming with other agencies and industry groups.

The General Environment for DoD M&S

Ultimately, the future of composability depends on having a favorable environment, one that includes a strong industrial base, incentives that promote sensible developments, and mechanisms that support technically sound and fair competitions among ideas and proposals. Standards, addressed above, are a key element here, but many other elements apply as well. These relate to issues such as existence of a marketplace of ideas and suppliers, mechanisms for configuration management and virtual repositories, incentives at the individual and organizational level, and a balance between maintaining long-term relationships with centers of excellence and assuring vitality with a constant inflow of ideas and challenges. In addition, it will be important to create a sense of community in appropriate segments of industry where close cooperation is sensible. This will also require incentives. One way for DoD to create incentives is to conduct evaluations of competitive weapon-system concepts in virtual environments that are as open as possible to all concerned, and that allow for component substitution if it can be demonstrated that one is better than another for a particular purpose.

Large-scale DoD M&S efforts would be well served by a much greater degree of commonality with the activities of the commercial sector. This would increase both options and dynamism, in part because it would enable good commercial-sector ideas, methods, and tools to be adapted quickly to defense applications. One possible element of "other infrastructure" would be technology and standards allowing rapid searches for potentially relevant components and allowing reasonably efficient zooming. These might include running candidates against standard datasets to see whether, at least superficially, the components do what the researcher imagines they will do. Evaluating possible compositions in the contexts of intended use automatically requires more cutting-edge developments, but movement in that direction is possible.

The Bottom Line

In summary, to improve prospects for composability in its M&S, **DOD must recognize that models are different from general software components and that model composability needs to be based on the science of modeling and simulation, not just on software practice. DoD should develop and communicate a set of realistic images and expectations, back away from excessive promises, and approach improvement measures as a system problem involving actions and investments in multiple areas ranging from science and technology to education and training.** Most of the investments could have high leverage if commercial developments are exploited; some will be more focused on DoD's particular needs.

Acknowledgments

We appreciate the many suggestions made at a workshop held on July 28, 2003, in RAND's Washington, DC, office and in subsequent communications with participants. Attendees were Jim Coolahan (Johns Hopkins University's Applied Physics Laboratory), Thomas Dufresne (OSD, Program Analysis and Evaluation), David Gross (Boeing Phantom Works), Henson Graves (Lockheed-Martin Aeronautics), Margaret Herald (Lockheed-Martin Aeronautics), Rich Ivnetich (Institute for Defense Analyses), Dwayne L. Knirk (Sandia National Laboratories), Duncan Miller (BBN and SISO), Steve Olsen (SM&S Inc.), Ernest Page (Army G3/Alion), Mikel Petty (Old Dominion University), Paul Reynolds (University of Virginia), Stuart Starr (MITRE), Andreas Tolk (Old Dominion University), Daniel Williams (Electric Boat Corp.), Eric Weisel (Werner Anderson), the authors (Robert Anderson and Paul Davis, of RAND), and Ken Atkinson (SAIC) and Doug Clark (GARD), of DMSO. Bernard Zeigler (University of Arizona) and Steve Hall (Lockheed-Martin Space Systems) were unable to attend but provided valuable comments separately. Annette Ratzenberger (previously of U.S. Joint Forces Command) shared with us many of her recent experiences with composition of model federations. Discussions with David Alberts (OSD/NII) reminded us to emphasize implications of networking. We also had a very informative meeting with Del Lunceford of the Army Modeling and Simulation Office. Although the DMSO staff sought our independent analysis and restrained themselves in commenting along the way, we nonetheless benefited greatly from the wide-open charge we were given and the help we received along the way. Finally, we acknowledge the substantive and constructive review comments received from RAND colleagues Louis Moore and Shari Lawrence Pfleeger, and the informal review comments of Jeff Rothenberg. While we greatly appreciate the many comments and suggestions that we received, the resulting monograph is our own responsibility. It is not intended as a consensus document, and it does not necessarily reflect the positions of anyone except the authors.

Acronyms and Abbreviations

ACOA	alternative course of action
ADL	architecture description language
ASP	acoustic sensor program
BAT	brilliant anti-tank
C4ISR	command, control, communications, computers, intelligence, surveillance, and reconnaissance
CAGIS	cartographic analysis and geographic information sytem
CCRP	Command and Control Research Program
CMSE	composable mission space environments
COI	community of interest
CORBA	common object request broker architecture
DAML	DARPA agent markup language
DARPA	Defense Advanced Research Projects Agency
DDDS	Defense Data Dictionary System
DEVS	discrete-event simulation
DIS	distributed interactive simulation
DMSO	Defense Modeling and Simulation Office
DSB	Defense Science Board
EEA	essential elements of analysis

HLA	high-level architecture
IDA	Institute for Defense Analyses
IER	information exchange requirement
ISR	intelligence, surveillance, and reconnaissance
JANUS	a simulation named after the Roman god Janus
JICM	joint integrated contingency model
JSIMS	Joint Simulation System
JWARS	Joint Warfare System
LoC	lines of code
LOCAAS	low-cost anti-armor submunition
M&S	modeling and simulation
M&SPCC	Modeling and Simulation Professional Certification Commission
MADAM	model to assess damage to armor by munitions
MC02	Millennium Challenge 2002
MDA	model-driven architecture
MEASURE	mission effectiveness analysis simulator for utility, research, and evaluation
ModSAF	modular semi-automated forces
MORS	Military Operations Research Society
MOVES	modeling, virtual environments, and simulation
MRMPM	multiresolution, multiperspective modeling
NPS	Naval Postgraduate School
OIL	ontology inference layer
OMT	object-model template
OneSAF	entity-level battalion and below constructive simulation with semi-automated forces
OOTW	operations other than war
OSD	Office of the Secretary of Defense

OSI	open systems interconnect
OWL	semantic markup language for publishing and sharing ontologies on the web, based on DAML+OIL and RDF
PEM	PGM effectiveness modifier; also precision engagement model
PGMM	precision-guided mortar munition
PGM	precision-guided munition
R&D	research and development
RDF	resource description framework
RJARS	RAND Jamming and Radar Simulation
RSAS	RAND Strategy Assessment System
RTAM	RAND Target Acquisition Model
RTI	run-time infrastructure
SADARM	seek and destroy armor
SAIC	Science Applications International Corporation
SAM	surface-to-air missile
SAS	statistical analysis system
SBA	simulation-based acquisition
SEDRIS	synthetic-environment data representation and interchange specification
SEMINT	seamless model interface
SES	system entity structure
SFW	sensor-fused weapon
SISO	Software Integration Standards Organization
TACM	tactical missile system
TGW/TGP	terminally guided weapon/projectile
TRAC	TRADOC Analysis Center
TRADOC	Training and Doctrine Command

UAV	unmanned aerial vehicle
UCAV	unmanned combat aerial vehicle
UML	unified modeling language
USJFCOM	U.S. Joint Forces Command
V&V	verification and validation
WAM	wide-area munition
WARSIM	Warfighters' Simulation
XMI	XML-based metadata interchange
XML	extensible markup language
XMSF	extensible modeling and simulation framework

CHAPTER ONE
Introduction

We have two objectives in this monograph: First, to suggest a framework for discussing the challenges and opportunities for model composability in the context of Department of Defense (DoD) applications, and second, to identify concrete efforts that might be taken to make further progress in this endeavor.

Definitions

We distinguish sharply among "model," "program," "simulation," "module," and "component." Appendix A discusses the definitions in more detail and relates our definitions to those used elsewhere. Briefly, however, our usage is as follows

A *model* is a representation of a system, entity, phenomenon, or process—the model's *referent.* A model may be implemented in different ways by different computer *programs* (e.g., programs written in different languages). A *dynamic model* describes the behavior of the referent over time. *Simulation* is the act of using a simulation engine (i.e., a *simulator*) to execute a dynamic model in order to study its representation of the referent's behavior over time. Simulation models and simulation programs are models and programs, respectively, used for simulation. An *experimental frame* is the set of conditions imposed on a given simulation experiment, e.g., the input values that will be considered, the outputs that will be monitored, and how those outputs will be used. The *validity* of a model (or its implementing program, or of a simulation experimenting with the model) should be judged with respect to a referent and an experimental frame. That is, does the model adequately represent the referent in the particular experiment, which involves a particular context and use?

Large models are usually best designed to be *modular*. That is, they have parts that can be independently developed and tested, parts that are seen by the rest of the model as "black-box" building blocks that can be interacted with only through the inputs and outputs of a well-defined interface such as ports. A *module* may be quite complex internally but still have a simple interface. A module's internal processes may or may not be reviewable by, comprehensible to, or changeable by someone composing a new system.

Large models always have *parts*, sometimes called *components*, which may simply be names for notional pieces that are not in fact independent modules. In this monograph, however, *components* are true modules. Moreover, components are suitable for reuse—not just in other parts of some original model, but elsewhere, and perhaps even by third parties. Informally, one may think of components as relatively portable building blocks.

Composability then, is the capability to select and assemble components in various combinations to satisfy specific user requirements meaningfully. A defining characteristic of composability is the ability to combine and recombine components into different systems for different purposes.[1]

Although advocates of composability often operate with an ideal of plug-and-play, we do not require plug-and-play as part of our definition. Indeed, assembling model components in a new way may require weeks or even months of significant rethinking and adjustment, even when some or all of the components being used are quite apt. Also, while advocates of composability and component-based work often emphasize that to be particularly valuable the components should be available in a "market" where competition can take place for both function and cost, we do not require that as part of our defi-

---

[1] This definition is that of Petty and Weisel, 2003, except that we added the term *meaningfully*.

nition. By and large, then, we have defined terms to make them inclusive, rather than exclusive, to encourage distinctions among types and degrees of composability.

Background

Impetus for the Study

The subject of model and simulation composability is hardly new. To the contrary, it has been discussed for decades, as reflected in the considerable related literature.[2]

The fact remains, however, that the aspirations of the Department of Defense (DoD) for composable systems have not usually been achieved, and there have been some notable disappointments. As a result, the Defense Modeling and Simulation Office (DMSO) asked the RAND Corporation to take a fresh look, one that could help guide a related DMSO-sponsored research and development (R&D) program. The office's starting point is described on its website (Defense Modeling and Simulation Office, 2002):

> Certainly we have some ability to "compose" simulations today (e.g., JSIMS, JWARS, MC02, etc),[3] but there are stumbling blocks regarding our ability to do this "rapidly," "flexibly" and efficiently. These stumbling blocks are not insurmountable, but we have discovered that unless models are designed to work together they don't (at least not easily and cost effectively). It is also believed that not all of the solutions will come from technology: many will come in the form of processes.

---

[2] For early technical discussions, see Dahmann and Woods, 1995, a special issue of the *Proceedings of the IEEE*. For an informal account of some of the heady days of early distributed interactive simulation, especially early-1990s work sponsored by the Defense Advanced Research Projects Agency (DARPA), see Neyland, 1997.

[3] JSIMS (Joint Simulation System) and JWARS (Joint Warfare System) are the result of large investments (on the order of $1 billion). Millennium Challenge 2002 was a very large and expensive distributed exercise conducted by the U.S. Joint Forces Command as part of transformation experimentation.

> The goal of DMSO's Composable Mission Space Environments (CMSE) initiative, sometimes referred to as "composability," is to identify the issues related to "composability" and then target DMSO initiatives (and related research from other organizations) . . . [and] lay the groundwork for increased reuse and the improved ability to compose simulations more rapidly, flexibly, and efficiently.

Consistent with this, DMSO urged RAND to open all doors, ask all questions, and provide a fresh assessment of composability issues. Although composite modeling and simulation (M&S) frequently involves hardware and human components, most of our focus in this monograph is on software in the form of models.

Is a Focus on Model Composability Desirable?

It became clear early in our research that a good deal of skepticism exists in the community about the desirability of *model* composability, at least as a major objective in development efforts. It is therefore appropriate to address this issue at the outset, rather than merely assuming that DoD interest in a subject necessarily implies its appropriateness. It was not long ago, after all, that DoD's passion seemed to be imposing the Ada language across the board. Could model composability be an equally dubious concept?[4]

Upon reflection, the answer is clearly No—at least with the broad definition of composability that we use. As mentioned in the definitions, modularity and composability are closely related. Modularity is *necessary* when dealing with complex systems, and some degree of composability is surely possible and desirable. There are a number of reasons. We present them here largely as assertions, but they will probably be convincing to most readers who are practitioners of modeling and simulation, and a substantial related literature exists on the subject. The reasons we emphasize relate to all phases of M&S:

---

[4] DoD mandated use of Ada in 1987. Following a recommendation from the National Academy (see National Research Council, 1997c), DoD dropped the mandate a decade later.

1. *Creating* a simulation of a large, complex system requires breaking the problem down into parts that can be addressed separately—to reduce the effects of interruption, to permit specialization, to facilitate computing alternative ways of handling a given component, to maintain the software over time, and to reduce risk by relying upon previously proven components where possible. Often, it is best that such parts be "modules."[5] Creating a system of systems is necessarily dependent on coupling such modules together.[6]
2. *Understanding* complex systems requires decomposition because no one can otherwise comprehend the whole's details—much less explain them.[7] How to decompose and whether one needs only one breakdown or many is always an issue, but the need for decomposition is well established.
3. *Testing* systems is vastly simplified if one can do it module by module, and then at the system level.
4. *Controlling M&S costs* is important, and those costs are strongly correlated with the amount of new code writing. The economic incentives for reuse, then, can be considerable. If a program has 3 million lines of code, which can be written at the rate of 75 lines per person-day, and each person-day costs $500, then the associated cost is $20 million. If even half of the program were a reuse of earlier code, the savings might be on the order of many millions, and the time to complete the program might be many months shorter. To be sure, however, reuse is not free. There are

---

[5] For a classic discussion of this, see Simon, 1981. The concepts of "coupled systems" and "systems of systems" are both familiar in today's world and depend upon and exploit concepts of modularity. See, for example, Zeigler, Praehofer, and Kim, 2000; Szyperski, 2002; and Sage and Cuppan, 2001.

[6] For a short discussion of what makes systems of systems unique, see Maier, 2002. See also Sage and Cuppan, 2001. For a visionary military discussion (parts of which have already been realized), see especially Owens and Offney, 2000. Other useful discussions include Hofmann, 2003, based on a recent dissertation; books on systems engineering, such as Sage, 1995; and Pfleeger, 2001. Kapustis and Ng, 2002, is a good issues paper.

[7] The importance to cognition of both abstraction and decomposition is discussed in Davis and Bigelow, 1998, and Bigelow and Davis, 2003.

significant costs entailed in understanding the components, modifying them to suit the new purpose, and documenting them as they evolve for the new application. Nonetheless, considerable cost savings can be realized if the composability feature is used multiple times.

5. *Maintaining and modifying M&S* are also greatly simplified with a modular construction: Individual modules can be substantively modified or updated as software as necessary, without endangering the overall system.[8] This is in contrast to the common situation in which an organization is afraid to improve a particular algorithm for fear that the whole system, written years earlier, will collapse.
6. *Using M&S* is also improved by modularity. For example:
   - Conducting distributed war games and exercises, which have come into their own in recent years, depends fundamentally on the ability to compose,[9] e.g., to combine ground-combat, aerospace, and naval models.
   - Preparing military forces for flexibility requires M&S flexibility so that different concepts and systems can be assessed or used in a wide range of operating circumstances. Such flexibility is at the heart of capabilities-based planning.[10]

Modularity, then, is good. As noted above, however, composability is more than modularity.

---

[8] Such maintenance of a modular construction scheme implies the need for configuration management, for example, to keep track when one module evolves in several different directions for differing purposes and all are stored within a common global (or corporate/organizational) repository.

[9] See, e.g., U.S. Joint Forces Command, 2002; for a more technical discussion of federation issues encountered, see Ceranowicz, Torpey, Helfinstine, Evans, and Hines, 2002.

[10] Capabilities-based planning has been mandated by DoD (see Rumsfeld, 2001; for a more analytic discussion, see Davis, 2002a).

What Should We Be Expecting of Model Composability?

Clarifying what types of composability are actually achievable and what types are especially valuable is very important.[11] With this in mind, many objectives often stated as part and parcel of composability should be scrutinized in a fresh look. Table 1.1 itemizes some of them. Some are dubious, but none are strawmen—we have heard all of them advocated vociferously by senior military officers and even by senior DoD officials over the past decade. Significantly, however, not all visionary goals are useful; some are downright counterproductive, as many of us learned when studying the dangers of utopian thinking in political philosophy. Many historical mathematicians would probably have agreed, having spent years of their lives trying to accomplish things that Gödel later proved to be impossible.[12]

Table 1.1
Some of the Many Hopes, Wise or Dubious, Associated with Composability

- A good composable approach should greatly reduce costs and allow us to do things once and get it "right." We don't need all the many models that now exist.
- We want to be able to turn the crank and know the results are authoritative because they're based on combining individually authoritative components.
- With plug-and-play, we won't need programmers all over the place and PhDs at every terminal of our exercises.
- We should be able to assemble the right system of systems with plug-and-play and answer tradeoff questions within weeks, perhaps operating with only a few analysts and a virtual environment of on-call consultants.
- This will enable inculcating forces with new joint doctrine by assuring that everyone works with authoritatively developed joint M&S.
- By having a vigorous commercial marketplace generating alternative components, we can have the benefits of competition in improving quality and reducing cost.

---

[11] In the same spirit of distinctionmaking, Nance (1999) has critiqued the desirability and feasibility of universal interoperability.

[12] Page and Opper (1999) describe formally some of the fundamental limitations of some people's visions for idealized composability.

Do we want to build any, some, or all of these objectives into the very definition of composability in the DMSO context? As implied by the definitions given above, the answer is No. Instead, *we consider composability as a matter of degree and context.* So also is the desirability of composability. Consider an experience that many readers have probably had. After reading a text or attending a course that stressed the virtue of always building programs in small modules, many have begun building a "real" model, only to find that the tedium associated with such a "requirement" simply doesn't pay its way. Instead, they found it faster, easier, and in some ways more elegant to build the program in a direct, unified way, without the boilerplate required for the rigorous modularity that assures that modules can be tested and run independently. The desirability of building for composability has something to do with scale and context.

Another experience that many have probably shared is that of having gone to the trouble to develop a component-ready model and its documentation, and then observing that in fact only work-group companions or some colleagues "down the hall" ever use the model, thereby suggesting that much of the extra effort was wasted. Companies with bottom lines in mind will not invest in composability unless they can see the corresponding system being used and adapted enough over time to justify the costs.

As for having a commercial marketplace of model components on which to draw, it remains unclear where that image applies. It is one thing to savor the marketplace of plug-in modules for software such as Microsoft Excel; it is another to imagine frequent shopping for major combat models, which take a great deal of time and effort to evaluate and, later, to learn. Table 1.2 gives examples of components that illustrate the enormous range of cases,[13] examples that

---

[13] Petty and Weisel (2003) describe eight levels of composability that were cited in the military literature they surveyed.

should reinforce the sense that achieving composability is a drastically difficult matter, depending on level of detail and other factors.[14]

There are, then, many cautionary anecdotes and logical reasons to suggest that we should contain enthusiasm for composability in general and instead look more deeply into precisely what is needed, what level of detail and in what context, how difficult it is to achieve, and where it would pay off most handsomely. That background of considerations has motivated the approach in the rest of this monograph.

Table 1.2
Illustrative Components at Different Levels of Detail

Component	An Illustrative Function
Terrain database	Represent 10-m digitized terrain, including roads and buildings, within a battle sector of a larger simulation.
Behavior	Represent how sortie-generation rate of an aircraft carrier battle group changes in response to tasking, prior preparation for surges, etc.
Object	Represent a particular type of tank in an entity-level simulation (e.g., JANUS) in which direct "physics-level" engagements occur. Object attributes might be at the level of single-shot kill probability versus range and type of target.
Unit-level object	A component representing a battalion in a higher-level simulation (e.g., JWARS) in which attrition is based on force-on-force calculations and movement of units is stereotyped with parameters (e.g., 100-m spacing along a road, maintaining a speed of 40 km/hr)
Air-forces model	Represent the operations of Air Force and Navy air forces in a larger theater-level model (e.g., JICM).
Federate	A component representing a major force element in a joint experiment, such as Millennium Challenge 2002.

[14] It is sometimes said that low-level components are easier to work with than high-level components. That is not necessarily true, because what matters is the complexity of the components and their interactions with others.

Shared, Accessible Data for Composability

One critical composability-related subject that we do not discuss in this monograph is the matter of data: creating, sharing, and reusing relevant databases on matters ranging from digitized terrain to characteristics of weapon systems. Many researchers involved with composability-related work emphasize that the data problem is one of the most important and most vexing issues. We have chosen to focus on model issues here, in part because of time limitations and in part because the data issue is significantly different from model issues. However, we include in Appendix C a brief summary of others' recommendations on data issues.

Approach

Setting aside the issue of data, our approach in the remainder of this monograph (Figure 1.1) is to review critically the very concept of composability and muse about what makes it difficult, in the process defining numerous distinctions discussed in Chapter Two; and then to draw on the insights from that exercise to move (in Chapter Three) to a set of tentative suggestions about how the DMSO and

Figure 1.1
Approach of This Monograph: Diverge to Understand Broadly, Converge to Suggestions

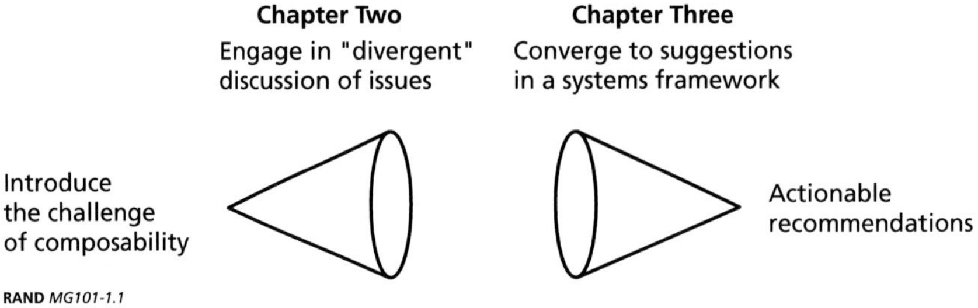

RAND *MG101-1.1*

other offices might work to improve the situation in a program of investments and priorities.

We have also included a number of appendices elaborating on particular issues.

- Appendix A provides definitions and related discussion.
- Appendix B is an essay about the subtleties of composability.
- Appendix C summarizes briefly the findings of a recent workshop on ways to improve data sharing and reusability.
- Appendix D is an extended discussion illustrating with a toy problem some of the more subtle substantive problems that arise in efforts to compose models and to characterize M&S at a high level.
- Appendix E describes two substantial examples of composability in practice, based on work at RAND and at Lockheed-Martin (Sunnyvale). Both focus on analysis, rather than on applications to training or operations.
- Appendix F summarizes some highlights of past work on simulation-based acquisition (SBA), primarily to note overlaps with this monograph.
- Finally, Appendix G summarizes comments received by us at the workshop mentioned earlier.

With this introduction, then, let us now turn to a review of the broad range of reasons for the difficulty of model composability.

CHAPTER TWO

Factors Affecting Composability

Initial Comments

The ability to compose models or simulations from diverse components obviously depends on the components themselves and on the context in which such composition takes place. In this chapter, we list a number of the factors that affect composability; these factors can be grouped compactly as in Figure 2.1. The list is broad, although surely not yet comprehensive. The initial version formed the basis for dis-

Figure 2.1
Assessing Prospects for Composability

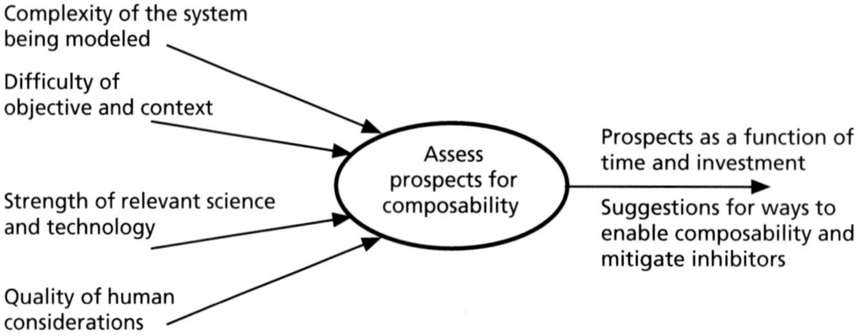

RAND *MG101-2.X*

cussion at the workshop noted above,[1] and what appears here is an iteration reflecting that workshop, review comments, and further thinking. Even so, the list is a beginning for discussion rather than an endpoint.

In the following sections, we discuss each of the factors, grouped in the four categories indicated in Figure 2.1: complexity of the system being modeled; complexity of purpose, context, and function for the M&S; strength of relevant science and technology; and strength of human considerations for the contemplated effort. Figure 2.2 shows a graphical breakdown. We have attempted to keep the various factors reasonably orthogonal, so that they can be discussed independently, even if some are correlated—in the sense, for example, that large models are more often than not complex models. Although other compositions are certainly possible, this one has proved useful for our purposes. Note that a number of factors along the lower right side of Figure 2.2 can be lumped together as "infrastructure." Also, a number of factors along the left side vary depending on the "nature" of the M&S application.

Notionally, if we understood the factors of Figure 2.2 well enough, we could quantify their effects and contribute to a science of composability by developing parametric plots of the risk of a composition effort versus aggregate versions of the factors. Figure 2.3 illustrates this idea. The figure is purely speculative but qualitatively reasonable. Risk rises with some measure of "effective" size and complexity, but it rises faster if the composite M&S will be used in rigorous analytic work (i.e., work in which variables must be tightly controlled, the work must be reproducible, and the results will be used to inform choice), and it rises extremely fast if any of several danger factors are present. These include poor management; the crossing of many military or cultural boundaries in attempting the composition; and a poor understanding of what is being modeled,

---

[1] The workshop was held on July 28, 2003, in RAND's Washington, DC, office. See the Acknowledgments for a list of participants and Appendix G for a distillation of comments.

Figure 2.2
Factors Affecting the Difficulty of M&S Composition

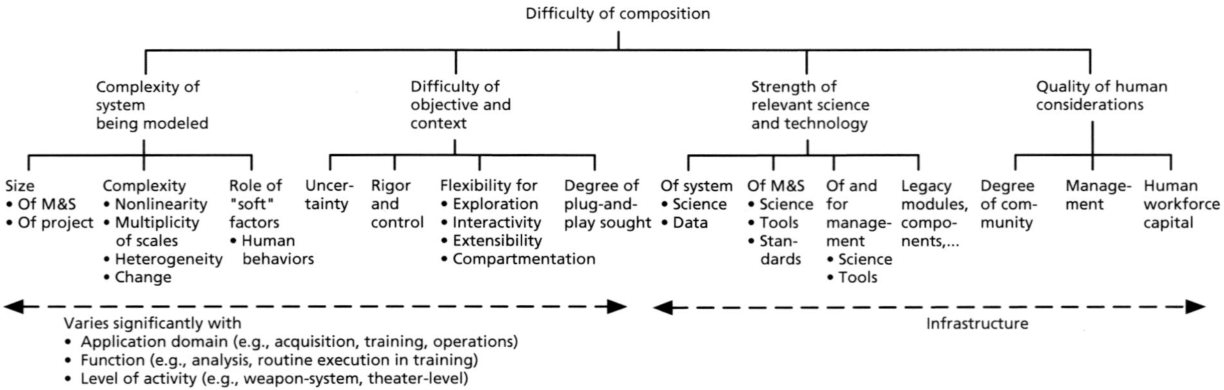

RAND *MG101-S.1*

Figure 2.3
Notional Parametric Plot of Project Risk Versus Various Key Factors

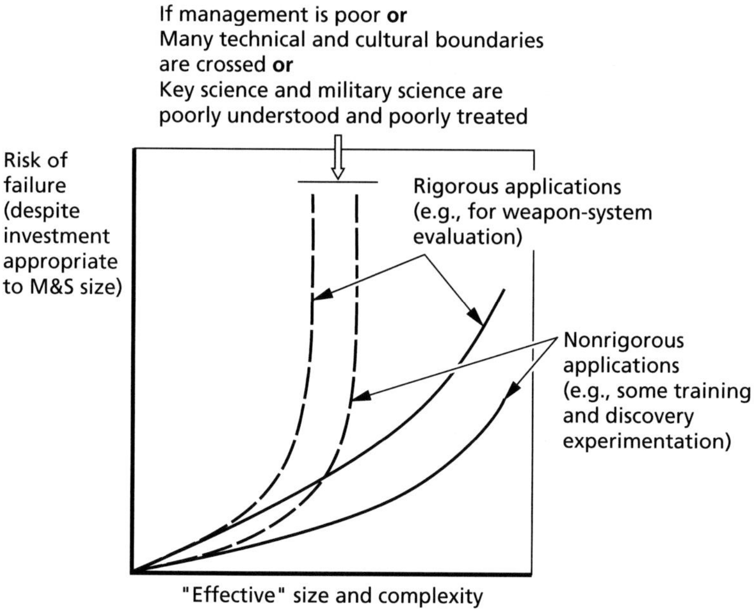

RAND *MG101-2.3*

worsened by a weak treatment of uncertainty. In these cases, the risk of failure is high even if expenditures are increased: These shortcomings cannot be overcome by simply throwing money at the problem. The groundwork has not been laid for even a rough quantification, but we seek to begin the journey by discussing the factors of Figure 2.2 in what follows.

Complexity of the System Being Modeled

The factors in the system-complexity category relate to the model or simulation itself: its size, the type of modules being composed, the phenomenology being modeled, and how well it is understood. This list is surely incomplete. Measuring the complexity of a model is not straightforward, and no agreed-upon framework for doing so exists. It should also be noted that complexity is a *relative* concept. This may not be immediately evident, but it becomes so when we consider something like the simplifying effect of using vectors and arrays in physics. Generations of scientists have expressed appreciation for the beauty and simplicity of Newton's and Maxwell's equations—when expressed in vector notation. They would not have done so had they been writing out the equations in scalar form.[2] Similarly, some conceptual models can be represented by simulations that are either more or less complex, depending on the programming language used. And, of course, for many problems, object-oriented modeling simplifies and clarifies a great deal.[3] As a final argument here, consider that even if one has a rich and excellent model of a natural phenomenon, it is *always* possible to add complexity by treating the phenomenon in more detail, thus again demonstrating that it makes sense to seek a measure of the complexity of a model or simulation, rather than only that of the phenomenon it represents.[4]

With these initial comments, let us now discuss eight measures of the complexity of the system being modeling.

Size of Model or Simulation

Size seems to limit the *potential* complexity of a model or simulation. One might consider measuring the size of a model or simulation in various ways, such as total lines of code in the composed system or number of modules or components being composed. However, the

[2] For an interesting history of developments between Hamilton's quaternions and the vectors introduced by J. Willard Gibbs in the late 19th century, see Vectors, an on-line resource guide (http://occawlonline.pearsoned.com/bookbind/pubbooks/thomas_awl/chapter1/medialib/custom3/topics/vectors.htm) that accompanies the classic calculus book by Thomas (2000).

[3] An excellent early book on this is Rumbaugh, Blaha, Blaha, Premerlani, and Eddy, 1990, notable in part because it deals with modeling, not just software. Rumbaugh's methods were one of the precursors to the unified modeling language (UML), which is discussed later and described at the website www.rational.com, among other places.

[4] This draws on Edmonds, 1999, a recent dissertation on syntactic complexity.

real issue here is less raw size than the number of factors that must be considered. Let us examine this in two parts.

Systems Engineering

If we think in systems-engineering terms, treating the model components as mere black boxes, one size-related measure of complexity is the number of distinct interface issues, parameters, or messages that have to be passed among the components. In system-of-systems interoperability, these have in the past been referred to as information exchange requirements (IERs), each of which defines something that has to be exchanged between a *pair* of systems. This measure is less apt today, as we are concerned increasingly with networked systems with many entities that may publish or subscribe items of information that may be used anywhere in the network[5]—if not today, then tomorrow, as the network and its entities evolve and adapt. In any case, a given item of information, whether in the form of an IER or a message to be published or received, involves both syntactic issues (data type, message length and protocol, etc.) and semantic issues (units and meaning of data, agreed-upon conventions for underlying algorithms and computational assumptions, etc.). Items of information also include issues of in-context validity.[6] The number of such items does not map exactly into lines of code, but it is related to the number of components and the complexity of each component's interface to the others. These two aspects could be combined. That is, a large component with a very simple interface to another would not add as many "interface points" as would a smaller component with a more complex interface.

A large number of simple modules could imply high complexity, since each such module would necessarily add at least one "interface

---

[5] For a discussion of military networking, see, e.g., Alberts, Garstka, and Stein, 1999; National Research Council, 2000; or U.S. Air Force Scientific Advisory Board, 1998. The latter is the "McCarthy study" on the joint battlefield infosphere. The National Research Council study was done for and influential in the development of the Navy's technical approach to network-centric operations.

[6] For a simple discussion of the differences among these, see Appendix A.

point," making the total number of such points high. But if many or all of these numerous modules shared the same interface points, e.g., many modules talking to each other about spatial position and using common conventions for computing and exchanging such positional information, then the complexity of their composition might be low. So a better metric is probably *distinct* interface points, where *distinct* means *either* syntactically *or* semantically distinct from other interface points. We therefore suggest that the total number and semantic complexity of distinct interface points among all of the relevant modules contribute to systems-engineering-level compositional complexity.[7]

Complexity Inside the Black Boxes

Continuing with this discussion, another issue is the number of points at which subtle issues of validity have to be dealt with, as when one component uses an output of another but it is not entirely clear whether the calculation of that information was valid for the purpose at hand. Here the count is not just at the interface between components. If an input to component A is generated by component B as a single well-understood datum, a good deal of work might still be required to check whether the datum's calculation was appropriate for the implicit assumptions of all the many places in component A in which that datum is used.[8]

---

[7] We are indebted to our colleague Jeff Rothenberg for this line of reasoning about appropriate metrics for "size" of a model or simulation (see also Appendix B). One of several other approaches discussed in the literature is the cyclomatic index discussed in Edmonds, 1999, which, roughly, counts the number of independent loops in the most economical graph possible of the model in the given representation. This is usually credited to McCabe (1976).

[8] As an example, suppose that component B computed the number of armored vehicles killed by air forces in a given time period. That number could be subtracted from the vehicle number resulting from that same time period's ground-force attrition. Syntax and semantics would be all right (as long as the concept of "kill" was consistent across the components). However, if the calculation by component B implicitly assumed that the effects of air forces were independent of the ground-force targets' state (e.g., static versus moving, moving on an open road versus moving in canopied terrain), then the validity of the number passed from component B to component A would vary with time in the course of the simulation. To discover this assumption of independence, one might need to look in some depth at the inputs and outputs, underlying algorithms, and buried databases. Regrettably, it is not unusual

This illustrates the need to look inside the black-box modules, rather than addressing only interface issues. Much of the real complexity of the composability problem—for models, rather than "pure software" components—relates to these inside-the-black-box issues. If the only issue were interoperability, and composability were not a concern, we might not care, but if the composition is supposed to be *meaningful* in the context of its application, then we must know enough about the innards of the modules to be sure that they do what we need, and do it well. Appendices A and B discuss related issues, including basic definitions and deeper matters involving semantics and validity. In characterizing the complexity of models, then, we must look deeper than interfaces, to what are sometimes called function points.

Implications. We assume that for small models or simulations, composability should usually be straightforward. For large programs, it is problematic, and although frameworks such as the high-level architecture (HLA) exist to assist the process at the systems-engineering level, composability is difficult to achieve—more of a *tour de force* than a routine scientific/engineering endeavor—and difficult to duplicate or replicate. For medium-sized programs, we might hope for a science of composability that achieves predictability, replicability, and a teachable, trainable discipline. That base of science would also help greatly on very large and complex efforts, but such efforts would still not be routine.

Research Issues. What is a good metric or set of metrics for the "effective size" of a model or simulation? Can one metric be used both for models and for simulations, or are the two sufficiently distinct that separate metrics should be used? Are distinct measures of size needed, depending on the underlying methodology used, such as agent-based programs, object-based programs, models described in

---

to see a complex model that appears to have allowed for all kinds of subtle factors, only to discover that in the database, the relevant arrays are trivial (with 0s in the cells for the various subtle factors).

UML,[9] C source code, and so on? How is success of composability correlated with size (as defined in this dimension) in real-world projects?

Size of M&S Project

Consider next the size of an M&S *project* or program, rather than the size of a model or simulation itself, discussed above. One might expect that project size would be correlated with the size of the M&S, but the relationship is not straightforward. After all, one could have a huge M&S with little content or complexity and with code almost entirely generated automatically. Or one could have a cutting-edge problem in which a large project is studying the phenomena, even though the resulting model and its components are modest in size. Thus, it makes sense to think about the factor of project size separately. Once again, the appropriate metric is not obvious: Number of people working on the project? Number of distinct offices or agencies involved? Length of chain of command from the project boss to the individual programmer? It is clear that composability for larger projects is more difficult, but what is the source of that increased difficulty?

Confusing matters further is the dependence of the *effective* size of the M&S project on other factors, notably (1) the quality of the architecture for composability in the project and of the substantive designs of the model components; (2) the quality of management; and (3) the number of communities involved, each with its own mental frameworks and semantics. The first two factors should be dealt with separately, in the sense that with "optimized" design and management, there would remain a residual effective size that would belong to this factor. The third factor, however, is special and, we believe, a likely culprit as a source of difficulty. We discuss some aspects of the community problem later (under Strength of Human Considerations), but a reasonable hypothesis is that the effective size of a project grows with the number of community boundaries that are

---

[9] Unified modeling language, a graphical method for describing models. It is a trademark of the Object Management Group (see http://www.omg.org/uml/).

crossed in accomplishing the composition. Each such boundary crossing requires special meetings, discussions, and iterations because of the difficulties involved in nailing matters down unambiguously. Why? Because the people involved do not share a fully common vocabulary and semantics, nor do they have the same tacit knowledge about the problem.[10]

Implications. Even if we take into account the size of the model itself, and even if we assume "optimal" design and management, some of the difficulty of M&S is related to project size.

Research Issues. It is unclear what an appropriate independent metric for an M&S project size is. Can this factor be teased out and made distinct from the other factors? What theoretical and empirical work, including review of past projects, would be useful here? What new empirical information might be sought, perhaps as a requirement of new DoD projects?

Degree of Nonlinearity

We use degree of nonlinearity as a measure of complexity in the sense associated with complex adaptive systems,[11] rather than, say, as a partial synonym for *difficulty* or *ignorance*. At the "uncomplex" end, there might be, for example, a set of linear models to be combined, such as a ground model that fights a Lanchester battle along a piston plus an air model that fights a separate Lanchester battle and affects the ground war only through a linear relationship between sorties and kills. To make things even more linear, such a model might treat the total ground-force attrition as simply the sum of the attrition caused by ground combat and air-to-ground operations.

---

[10] This is related to classic engineering disasters in an essay by John Doyle of CalTech (see Doyle, 1997).

[11] A good starting point for the rich literature on complex adaptive systems is Holland, 1995. A more recent book focuses on emergent phenomena (Holland, 1998). Within the military realm, one of the important applications of related thinking is in *effects-based operations*, which was seen by many as a mere fad a few years ago, but which has become a key element of modern thinking about command and control. See Deptula, 2001; Smith, 2003; and Davis, 2001a.

At a mid-level of complexity, there are nonlinear processes that have fixed algorithms but difficult-to-predict behavior and many interrelationships.

At a high degree of complexity, multiple levels of phenomena could be under way, with entities (human or otherwise) that adapt and perhaps morph, arise, or die off in the course of a simulation. Such variable-structure systems may require dynamic composability.[12] They may also show what are referred to as *emergent behaviors*, where phenomena at different levels appear to follow their own laws, which are not intuitively obvious from the laws of the next level down.[13]

Implications. As the degree of complexity in a module increases, there is the possibility of subtle and even emergent behaviors that were unforeseen initially and that are incompatible with existing in-

---

[12] A real-world referent might be a battlefield commander creating a new type of hybrid unit, drawing in part upon the unscathed portions of units that have suffered attrition and attaching a small unit normally assigned elsewhere. That hybrid unit may not even have been conceived before the war. In simulations, there are degrees of dynamic composability. For example, input data may define templates for units or operations that may or may not be created in the course of the simulation, using whatever simulated resources are available at that point. Or an entity may change its identity or attributes at some point, shifting from one preconceived set to another. Or, in interactive or interruptible simulations, wholly new structures can be inserted. Dynamic composability is common in entertainment games. See Singhal and Zyda, 1999.

[13] See Page and Opper, 1999. Consider also the following speculative case. Suppose that the close-combat attrition component of a ground-force model was constructed using a Lanchester square law. That component is used, along with a maneuver model and a command-control model, to form a composition. In the composed model, however, one of the forces disperses into rough terrain, and the other force must search through the terrain looking for battle opportunities. Instead of the homogeneous force-on-force battle for which the attrition model was originally intended, the simulation is now describing a more complex process. The individual real-world battles might possibly be described by a Lanchester square law, but the more macroscale phenomenon would look more like a Lanchester linear process because the rate at which battles would occur would depend on the force levels of *both* sides. Indeed, if one side were systematically benefiting from cover, then the governing equations would properly be asymmetric in structure, as described decades ago by Deitchmann (1962), who made empirical comparisons with Vietnam experience. In such an instance, then, combining several model components that seemed straightforward enough (one for attrition, one for command and control, and one for movement) would cause the character of the higher-level phenomenon to look quite unlike that of more-microscopic phenomena that had been built in (see National Research Council, 1997a).

terfaces and "contracts" among the modules that make up a simulation.

Research Issues. What are the metrics by which the degree of complexity in a module, or in the resulting composed model or simulation, should be measured? Which types of dynamic composability make composability more or less difficult? What can be learned from past examples of emergent behavior in complex simulation modules that was unanticipated and that complicated or thwarted the execution or use of a larger, composed simulation of which that module was a part?[14]

Number of "Horizontal" Components

A *horizontal* composition of models might be considered to be one involving modules that are approximately "at the same resolution." For example, a battlefield simulation might be created by a composition involving a terrain/geography module, a weather module, a ground campaign, and an air war (among others). This factor measures the number of such components that must be composed into a larger model or simulation. As the number of horizontal components *required* for the model increases, so also, presumably, does complexity.

Implications. It might be thought that a horizontal composition is "easier" than one involving substantially different levels of resolution (see next section), but such horizontal compositions often bring together different domains (i.e., "communities"), leading to problems of differing semantics. Also, the time domain may differ radically among horizontal modules. For example, ground models may be time-based with a relatively coarse time-step; they may entirely miss relevant events that occur in an air model, with its much finer-grained modeling of the time dimension. And, quite often, the components are actually wrapped models, the innards of which are not

---

[14] People disagree about how to define and recognize *emergent phenomena*, but we consider as examples the nonmonotonic and bizarre behaviors (sometimes reported as "chaotic" and sometimes referred to in terms of "structural variance") observed in combat models during the 1990s. For a review, see Speight, 2003.

fully understood by those doing the composing. Even if the components were developed, tested, and documented "reasonably," there might be substantial errors involved in combining them naïvely (see Appendix D, which illustrates problems in some detail with a simple example).

Research Issues. What are the confounding factors involved in horizontal composition of modules? Do the facilities provided by frameworks such as DoD's high-level architecture (HLA) address those complications, or are other facilities needed?[15] What standards, tools (e.g., for testing compositions in contexts different from those for which components have been developed), or best practices might mitigate the known problems of using wrapped models as black boxes during composition efforts?

Multiplicity of Scales and Need for Multiresolution M&S

A *vertical* composition involves modules at different resolutions or levels of detail. The example often used is that of the need in composite simulations to represent corps, divisions, brigades, battalions, companies, squads, and individual entities. Different components may be developed for each. But how do they relate? What should happen when a battalion (an abstraction that might ordinarily be described with force-on-force equations and average movement rates) encounters a group of individual armored vehicles generated by another component? There is no school solution to such issues because there is a fundamental mismatch and a need to introduce approximations, the appropriateness of which depends sensitively on context. Although one might think that the problem could be avoided by simulating everything at the highest level of detail, that notion is fun-

[15] The high-level architecture specifies interface requirements and other ground rules promoting reuse and interoperability in simulation activities. It has played a crucial role in recent years' distributed war games and experiments, perhaps most notably in the Millennium Challenge 2002 experiment conducted by the U.S. Joint Forces Command. Merely as an example of what ground rules are like, a tank object participating in an HLA-moderated confederation would be responsible for detecting and shooting at another target, but the rule is that the results of its round hitting that target would be determined by the target object, not the shooter. For information, see www.DMSO.mil or, e.g., Andrews, 1998.

damentally flawed even if there were no problem with the computational power needed.[16] The best way to understand this is to look at real life, where we constantly rely upon models at different levels of resolution just to cope moment-to-moment. A military commander, for example, may have enormous levels of detail available to him, but in thinking about his options and directing operations, he uses much more abstracted concepts (e.g., "move the 2nd brigade to the western side of the zone") than those relevant to lower-level commanders. On the other hand, this same commander may be sensitive to the status and well-being of individual high-value aircraft, communication links, or personally trusted lieutenants.

To make things worse, the concept of "resolution" is actually a crude abstraction in itself. In reality, composite simulations may have to deal with multiple resolutions of many different types, such as time, terrain, and level of organization. Moreover, the appropriate resolution for a given component may depend on context—for example, days of supply may in some cases be an adequate metric for summarizing a massive amount of logistics detail, while in other cases it is necessary to distinguish among supplies of artillery shells, precision munitions, and so on.

Software cannot solve these vertical problems. Rather, they are inherently challenges for the models themselves, challenges that will not go away, because of complexities in the real world. Furthermore, the need to have models at differing levels of resolution, and reflecting different perspectives, is *fundamental* for decision support and many types of analysis. One reason is that to understand and explain what is going on in complex high-resolution simulations, we usually need abstractions. A second reason is that in dealing with massive uncertainty, it is often preferable to conduct exploratory analysis at a high level (low resolution), whereas high resolution is essential to understand the intricacies of phenomena.

---

[16] This discussion draws on Davis and Hillestad, 1993, and Davis and Bigelow, 1998. The Air Force Research Laboratory has sponsored work on model abstraction that appears in yearly *SPIE* conferences. For a short summary with citations as of the late 1990s, see Sisti and Farr, n.d.

Implications. One implication is that where one crosses levels of detail in simulations, as in composing modules developed separately or even in composing modules developed by a single organization desiring a multilevel depiction, it is essential to understand the military science in doing so and to then represent that knowledge in programs. The common approach of merely postulating a simple aggregation or disaggregation relationship often does violence to the underlying phenomena, as, for example, when a modeler makes the naïve but convenient assumption that both sides of a ground-force battle are able to employ reserves optimally.

Composability can seldom be a matter of plug-and-play in the vertical direction(s) unless—most unusually—the modules in question were designed to operate together from the outset, as in multiresolution modeling or the related use of integrated model families.

Research Issues. By military subject area and context of use, what are the valid ways of aggregating and disaggregating? What approximations are reasonably accurate yet simplify relationships substantially so as to enable cross-calibration across levels? When should input variables that are formed as abstractions be represented stochastically, deterministically with uncertainty ranges, or as point values? What are relevant metrics for determining the degree of compatibility in resolution among different would-be components? Can the resulting metrics be used to help predict the success and efficiency of a desired composition? For all of these, what tools would help?

The Importance of "Soft Factors"

One of the increasingly well-recognized difficulties in modeling, and presumably in composition, is that of dealing with "soft factors." This phrase usually relates to human decisions and other behaviors that are notoriously difficult to predict. However, the phrase is also sometimes used in connection with uncertainty-related squishiness of problems. If we think of a spectrum of squishiness, at one end are models that represent well-understood physical systems such as missile trajectories. At the other end are models that are importantly influenced by soft factors. They may not be inherently complex in the sense of operational behavior ("the target may either engage or run away, and we haven't the faintest idea which"), but they may be very difficult to model well, much less predictively. Moreover, resulting models may be less than rigorous or comprehensive.

Implications. Poorly understood soft-factor processes, perhaps represented by sets of heuristic rules, may be less composable within larger assemblages because not all of their behaviors, in all circumstances that might arise within the model or simulation, can be foreseen and treated clearly. Also, such behaviors tend to have many more tacit dependencies on the context of the situation, and therefore many more entanglements with other modules. As with expert systems, issues here include completeness, explainability, and brittleness.

Research Issues. What are the principles for creating component models dealing with soft-factor phenomena such as human decisions and behaviors? How do they differ from principles for more "physical" components? More broadly, what are the principles for creating and using component models dealing with squishy phenomena in the sense of large uncertainties?[17] What is the theory for understanding how uncertainties propagate as a result of composition? When do they expand or even explode, and when do they contract? What can be done to control this?[18]

Subject-Area Heterogeneity of Natural Components

Some composite models involve components that are naturally expressed in very different representations and formalisms because the phenomena are different in character. Missile trajectories are best represented by continuous differential equations, whereas force-on-force

---

[17] We suspect that a key here will be a best practice that attaches a database for routine parametric variation of the uncertain parameters, perhaps in a manner facilitating "exploratory analysis" in which the variations are made simultaneously rather than one at a time around some imagined best-estimate point. See, e.g., Davis, 2002a, and references therein.

[18] As an example, many military component models are implicitly intended to be used for short periods of time. They may, however, be composed with others and run for much longer periods. Depending on the experimental frame used for the analysis (which might, for example, limit the time period) and the nature of command-and-control processes (which might, for example, "clear the slate" fairly often, stopping the uncertainties from propagating further), the meaningfulness of simulated outcomes might be much higher or lower.

ground battles lend themselves well to discrete-event simulation or time-stepped simulation with large time steps. There are also differences in granularity, i.e., differences in number and kinds of aspects. This need for heterogeneity is not merely an artifact of the mathematics or programming. A standard problem faced by commanders is that their natural command-and-control times for major decisions can be discrete (e.g., once a day), whereas the course of events may change within a much shorter time scale. Delays in reacting can be quite troublesome. Another example that comes to mind is the difference between the "natural" way to describe the approach of a low-flying, low-signature antiship cruise missile and the approach of a squadron of enemy aircraft that will be encountered in air-to-air combat. The former might require high-data-rate tracking because the ability to engage a cruise missile is marginal and dependent on sensor and weapon performance over very short periods of time. In contrast, tracking a squadron of enemy aircraft could be done with a much lower data rate. Such differences underlie the continuing difficulties in achieving interoperability of command-and-control systems.

At times, modules making up a composition might be homogeneous in their design or implementation—for example, all represented in unified modeling language (UML) notation (if the model's characteristics can all be described within such a notation), or in C++, or in some object or agent system. Other collections of modules might be congeries of differing designs, implementation languages, and standards. Various frameworks, notably the high-level architecture (HLA), have been designed to mitigate the problems of certain types of heterogeneity among modules, but much more work is needed.

Implications. We assume that homogeneity makes things easier when one is attempting a complex composition of modules. At minimum, greater heterogeneity requires a greater skill set among the composability team, as well as a larger set of concepts and notations to be adjudicated. The difficulty could be reduced if there were an intermediate, common, transitional interface with which differing modules could be interfaced, but none exists in most cases.[19]

Research Issues. What science and technology are most needed to make progress in dealing with heterogeneous components? Can the degree of homogeneity or heterogeneity be measured? If so, by what scale? How can we characterize existing composability projects by the degree of homogeneity of their modules? Is this correlated with success, as measured by reduced development time or accuracy and validity of results?

Changeability (or, Conversely, Stability) of Model Components

One of the primary motivations for composability in M&S is reuse of components. However, the objects or processes being modeled may not be very stable (i.e., they may be subject to substantial change). In that case, modules representing these objects or processes may have so short a shelf-life that designing and constructing for reuse is not worthwhile. Thus, changeability/stability is an important factor.

The scale of this factor is basically time. Some components, such as trajectory-calculation modules written in FORTRAN, might have an essentially infinite lifetime and may be indefinitely reusable. Others, such as a simulation of the characteristics of a novel, one-of-a-kind weapon system, might have a shelf life of weeks or months at most, because the characteristics of the modeled system are changing too substantially to be captured by simple parameterization. The same problem exists when dealing with candidate types of new military units.

Implications. In this era of military transformation, rather fundamental characteristics of military units, joint and combined-force operations, and weapons are changing substantially. It is not clear whether existing models or simulations of DoD-related units and activities can keep up with these changes, or whether those existing models must be scrapped and new ones created. If the latter is the

---

[19] Some of these issues were discussed by Paul Fishwick, Hans Vangheluwe, Paul Davis, and others in a recent Dagstuhl workshop (see papers in Fujimoto et al., 2002).

case, then there will be less call for composability, because there will be fewer modules on the shelf that are relevant to the new situation.

Research Issues. What are the expected shelf lives of a representative set of modules or components that might be candidates for reuse in future federations or compositions? How could shelf life be substantially increased (perhaps by more creative forms of parameterization)? What level of effort is justifiable for turning candidates into true components for reuse? Related to these questions, for those modules that must evolve, how can the evolution be controlled and documented so as to enhance composability?[20]

Complexity of Purpose, Context, and Function

Complexity of purpose, context, and function involves the context within which the model or simulation is being composed and used. The traditional breakdown might ask about the application area (e.g., acquisition, training, or operations) or the function being served by M&S (e.g., analysis versus repetitive training). However, such breakdowns seem motivated by organizational rather than technical considerations. So also, the breakdown by level (e.g., the strategic, operational, tactical, engagement, or "physics" level) does not work well for our purposes. All of these categories fall apart under closer scrutiny. For example, the category of "acquisition" applications includes such different activities as early exploration and experimentation, higher-level design, detailed design and specification setting, procurement, and testing. These contexts pose very different demands on M&S. Training is also a very mixed category, since some training is relatively loose and even free-form, while other training is careful, rigor-

[20] The importance of addressing the fact that useful software evolves was discussed in a well-known 1980 paper by Meir Lehman (1980), who distinguishes among S, P, and E systems: S (specifiable) systems represent "correct" solutions of stable systems; P (problem-solving) systems are approximate solutions to problems and are likely to change continuously as the approximations change for various contexts, and as the world being modeled changes; E (embedded) systems are embedded in the real world and change as the world changes, with both the system and the real world affecting each other.

ous, and repetitive. Even military operations is a very heterogeneous category, as illustrated by the differences among identifying and assessing broad campaign concepts; meticulously developing an air operations plan with concerns about air defenses, deconfliction, and fratricide avoidance; and a tactical commander's assessing, perhaps in a matter of minutes, immediate courses of action. As for level, the composability of a model depends on size, complexity, component stability, the role of soft factors, etc., rather than level per se.[21] *Simple* strategic-level models can be as composable as simple models at the level of radars and target detection.

What, then, should we use as factors to characterize context? There is no agreed framework for those factors, but we have used the following, which are intentionally technical and admittedly unusual: types and levels of uncertainty, the degree of control needed, the types and degree of flexibility needed, and the degree of plug-and-play intended. These factors all cut across the more usual categories mentioned above.

Uncertainty About Input Parameters and Data

Uncertainty is quite a different matter from complexity, as discussed in the previous section. Regardless of a model's size, complexity, and other attributes, there is a sense in which the model is only as good as the quality of inputs it receives. Quality of work, however, can be achieved by accuracy or by uncertainty analysis. Accuracy is relevant, for example, in dealing with databases for terrain, ocean properties, the presence of satellites in different trajectories, or the physical attributes of a new weapon system. If the databases used are poor, re-

---

[21] This can be seen in the distinctions for composition discussed in Petty and Weisel, 2003. They refer to applications, federates, packages, and parameters, modules, models, data, entities, and behaviors. What they treat as high level, however, happen to be large, complex, heterogeneous, and so on. And what they treat as low level are relatively simple. It is one thing to connect modest library-function mathematical subroutines (e.g., calculating a standard deviation) or somewhat more-complicated programming functions (e.g., sorting routines). It is quite another to combine modules of increasingly great scope and complexity (e.g., Air Force, Navy, and Army simulations, each with 10^5 lines of code and dozens to hundreds of submodels). All of this said, it is not really the level that matters in determining the difficulty of composing.

sults may suffer. If the models and data are good, predictiveness may also be good. In other cases, uncertainty analysis is the way to achieve quality. Many applications of M&S, after all, deal with problems beset with factors that are either unknown or even unknowable, not because of a lack of science, but for other reasons. Military options are often evaluated across a range of highly speculative future scenarios or across a range of possible enemy responses in a current conflict. The issue then becomes whether the uncertainty analysis is appropriately conducted, rather than whether any single run of a model is reliably predictive.[22]

Special issues arise in composability. In particular, each model (when taken together with its input data) is uncertain, and uncertainties may propagate in troublesome and nonintuitive ways.[23] Often, the team performing the composition has little of the information needed to assess such possibilities, and experimentation is confounded by a lack of explanation capability. That is, simulation outcomes are hard to understand.

Another common composability problem is a confounding of errors or uncertainties in the model and data, the simulator, and the manipulation of model output in the context of an application. Currently, it is relatively unusual for M&S compositions to be conducted within a framework that clearly disentangles these elements.[24]

---

[22] For more information on capabilities-based planning and model validation, see Davis, 2002a; and Bigelow and Davis, 2003.

[23] To illustrate how details matter here, consider how small uncertainties in the ground-force attrition-rate coefficients could propagate over the course of a 30-day war fought in a composite simulation with an air war, a ground war, long-range missiles, and interactions. In some compositions, the resulting uncertainty of output would dominate the analysis. In other instances, as when human players or automated command-control machinery is at work, this propagation might be relatively unimportant because, perhaps once a day, the simulated commanders would make large decisions about which battles to pursue, which ones to disengage from, and so on. Those might (or might not) wipe the slate clean with respect to propagation of errors about a particular battle. A realistic commander model would not, for example, continue to send outnumbered forces to certain death (although some cold-war theater-level models may do precisely that).

[24] These issues are emphasized in Zeigler, Praehofer, and Kim, 2000, and early chapters of Cloud and Rainey, 1998. See also Figure A.1 and related discussion in Appendix A.

Implications. It is important in any model composition project to understand the type and degree of uncertainty in the inputs, to understand how that uncertainty will propagate through the computations within the modules and through their linked input/output paths, and to understand how much accuracy is enough (or what kind of uncertainty analysis is appropriate) for the given application.

Research Issues. How should the type and degree of uncertainty in inputs be measured and reported? How should the resulting types and degrees of uncertainty in component outputs be measured and reported? How should a team contemplating or experimenting with a composition diagnose and evaluate issues of errors and error propagation? What tools are needed to facilitate these activities? What kinds of metadata and related standards might be useful? What can be done to improve model explanations, either in new models or in old ones?

Degree of Control Needed

Depending on the application, the user of a model may need to have precise and rigorous control over initial inputs, the resulting simulation dynamics, interactions (e.g., with a human team at one position of a game-structured simulation), etc. For some training applications (and also for some acquisition-related applications such as concept development), the level of control can be modest: One is "exploring," "experimenting," "learning by doing," and so on. In these applications, rigor is not particularly important or desirable; nor is exact reproducibility. Composition for such applications (as in many distributed war games using the high-level architecture (HLA) or the earlier distributed interactive simulation (DIS) protocol) is much easier and more forgiving than composition for rigorous analysis such as the evaluation of a weapon system or the assessment of certain courses of action in a real war, where getting details correct matters.

Implications. The difficulty of composition depends on the degree of control needed in the application, something that should be understandable if one has defined an appropriate experimental frame and has appropriately separated the concept of real system (referent), model, simulator, and experimental frame, as discussed in Zeigler, Praehofer, and Kim, 2000.

Research Issues. How should requirements for control be expressed by users, and how should the degree of control available in a component or composition be documented? Where high levels of control are needed, how should the component-level and composition-level specifications be expressed (distinguishing appropriately among model and data, simulator, and experimental frame)? Given that different applications require different levels of control, what implications should this have for standards, such as a given run-time infrastructure (RTI) consistent with the HLA?

Types and Degrees of Flexibility

Exploration

Some models and simulations are used repetitively in a narrow domain, while others are used to explore concepts, for discovery experiments, for preliminary high-level design, and for other applications requiring great flexibility, which may be provided with a combination of parameterization, alternative structures, alternative databases, and so on. Composability may be very helpful for exploration, but many component models—especially those provided with wrappers and no access to source code (to the black-box internals)—also limit, perhaps in subtle ways, what kinds of exploration are possible and valid.

Interactivity

A related issue is the degree to which the M&S should be interactive. Interactivity is, of course, a central feature of many training and gaming activities. In contrast, traditional, hard-core analysts have historically looked down upon interactivity, associating it with nonrigorous and nonreproducible human gaming. In our view, this has been a mistake, one that has led to unfortunate requirements such as that the JWARS model be closed (not interactive).[25] In contrast, other

[25] A closed simulation is run by "pushing a button," after which the simulation proceeds without human intervention. An interruptible simulation permits or demands human inter-

analysts have long seen interactiveness as crucial in order for simulations to be realistic and creative. Human teams may provide decisions as critical points; they may even develop new strategies different from what modelers had previously thought of. Ideally, M&S would be *optionally* interactive, or at least interruptible, with automated models available to do the same functions human players do. Building such features into a model is nontrivial, however, and building such features into a composition may be much more difficult because the components may not have been designed with that in mind or may have been designed with a different concept of how interaction should be accomplished.[26]

Extensibility

An important way to increase the flexibility of a model is to develop it in a way that is extensible, i.e., so that it can be adapted easily to include new features. This might mean new kinds of entities, new attributes for existing entities, new forms of interactiveness, and so on. Extensibility is strongly influenced by model design, programming language, composability-related protocols, the larger simulation environment, and probably other factors. Dynamic composability, for

---

vention at a discrete number of points, which may be determined by time, state, or event. Usually, an interactive simulation is assumed to be one that demands extensive human inputs during the course of events, but that need not be the case if one has automated models to substitute for humans if desired. The classic analogy here is that one may play chess with a human opponent or an automated model. Today, commercial war games often have devilishly clever adversary agents. The RAND Strategy Assessment System (RSAS) was designed so that human players could be used optionally in playing Red, Blue, or third parties. It had artificial-intelligence models that could be used instead, often as the result of observing human play and building corresponding automated strategies (see Davis and Winnefeld, 1983, or Davis, 1990). In analytic applications such as the RAND work described in Appendix E (see Matsumura, Steeb, Gordon, Herbert, Glenn, and Steinberg, 2001), a poor-man's version of this is accomplished by building scripts that reproducibly automate what has previously been observed as smart play by human operators, but without adaptation.

[26] If, for example, the structure of a module can be changed by a simulation's user during execution, this might have complicating implications for the set of contracts and linkages binding that module to others in a composed simulation. Even parameter changes might violate some existing understandings or contracts among the set of modules that constitute the simulation.

example, is currently not possible within the present implementation of the HLA.

Compartmentation

In some compositions, all of the information required by all parties is openly available to all. This information can be used to create a shared semantics and community and to negotiate contracts linking the inputs and outputs of various modules. In other DoD-related compositions, some modules may require classified or compartmented information and therefore must be treated to some extent as black boxes whose content is restricted.

We assume that open, shared information across modules (including knowledge of both their construction and their input/output interfaces) contributes to success in composability, since clarifications and misunderstandings can be resolved in a straightforward manner. In contrast, if some modules' assumptions or inner designs are restricted, misunderstandings might remain that would be undetected, thereby compromising the results of a composed model or simulation.

On the other hand, it might be assumed that individual modules *should* be treated as black boxes, to prevent users from inappropriately relying on their internal details or implementations; this has many advantages, such as allowing components to be revised or replaced without any impact on their users (as long as their contracts remain in force).

Implications. The flexibility of model components and a composable environment constitute a major issue, and the difficulty of achieving good and valid compositions will depend significantly on the types and degrees of flexibility sought.

Research Issues. For each of the above (and possibly for other dimensions of flexibility), what are the appropriate ways to specify, measure, document, and discuss the factors? How much is enough, as a function of the type of application and experimental frame?

Degree of Plug-and-Play Sought

One ideal of composability is that it be possible to compose by merely combining components that "plug and play together." This is possible in limited domains. For example, a number of simulation-building tools exist, e.g., for factory-floor simulation, that allow the user to construct a variety of modules by manipulating icons and filling in data; the resulting components will plug and play unless errors have been made. It is a much bigger stretch to compose by combining components developed in different projects, organizations, and contexts. If one seeks and greatly emphasizes the goal of plug-and-play, disappointment is likely. On the other hand, if sufficient time is allotted for review, adaptation, experimentation, and iteration, then much may be possible (including development of "wrappers" that modify the form of a component's outputs to permit them to be inputs to the desired component). Also, sharing in a plug-and-play sense is made more feasible (or the time required to tailor, experiment, and iterate is shortened) if the overall effort, including development of the components, has been accomplished within a sound systems-engineering activity.

Implications. Plug-and-play should not be part of the *definition* of composability, because that would label as "noncomposable" sets of components that could easily be connected sensibly with some new programming. On the other hand, developing components with plug-and-play or minimum tailoring in mind will likely pay high dividends where it is suitable (e.g., in relatively simple atomic models or objects for use within models). Waiting until the time of attempted assembly to think about the subtleties of syntax, semantics, and in-context validity is unwise, to say the least.

Research Issues. Are there predictors of the amount of tailoring of modules needed for a particular composition? Can the amount be estimated when such tailoring may require more effort than just creating modules from scratch? If so, on what basis? To what extent can the difficulties here be reduced by attaching good *and thoughtful* documentation to components as they are developed?

Strength of Relevant Science, Technology, and Legacy M&S

This category comprises factors related to the underlying basis of science and technology for the system being modeled and for the M&S tools and techniques used. It involves trying to measure how firmly grounded in science and technology are all aspects of the attempt to model a system and to perform composition of a number of separate modules.

Science and Technology for the System

The science and technology factor is somewhat related to the complexity of the system being modeled. It asks whether the scientific and technological principles underlying the system being modeled are accurate, sufficient, and understood. If they are, then it should be possible to form agreements on the meaning (semantics) represented within the modules to be composed, and therefore to document them well and agree on the meaning of the content to be exchanged across module interfaces. Further, it should be possible to assess in-context validity. Where the science is inadequate, even very clever modeling and programming may not accomplish much.

One aspect of all this is general science and technology—e.g., knowledge of atmospheric physics, kinetic laws, and electromagnetic interference—and the existence of tools and devices of various sources. Another aspect is military science, such as how best to configure and operate military units in today's world. Both of these continue to evolve (e.g., nanotechnology may revolutionize aspects of surveillance), but it is the military science about which we are most concerned in this monograph.

Implications. If models and simpuations can be no better than our knowledge of what they represent, the difficulty of meaningful M&S compositions will depend on that base of knowledge. This may be expressed in many different ways, including equations, logic statements, algorithms, and other notations upon which documentation and interface agreements can be shared and comprehended by all parties relevant to the M&S composition effort.[27]

Research Issues. How should the degree of science and technology underlying the target system be measured? Do modules based on some aspects of science and technology (e.g., physics of tank versus tank interaction) lead to better chances for composability than others (e.g., force-on-force-level models depicting maneuver and attrition of abstractions such as battalions and divisions)? If so, which? Where are the most serious shortcomings of military science?

Science-and-Technology-Related Knowledge, Tools, Policies, and Standards for M&S

There is a growing science of modeling and simulation. It involves understanding of appropriate languages and notations for expressing models (e.g., UML, DEVS[28]), structural alternatives (agent-based models, object-orientation, etc.), and appropriate frameworks (e.g., HLA) within which to perform composition of disparate modules. This monograph, in fact, is an attempt to extend the science of modeling by isolating the key factors that affect the success of M&S efforts involving the composition of separate modules.

Part of the issue, however, is technological "infrastructure." The term *infrastructure* covers a great deal of territory (arguably, all of the factors in this section and the next, as suggested by Figure 2.1), including the policies, standards, and processes by which work is contracted and accomplished; processes for verification, validation, and accreditation; and processes for routine and special-purpose development of databases. Many other examples could be listed, but these should suffice to make the point that the cost and quality of DoD's simulation activities depend heavily on a base that can be seen as infrastructure. Since large-scale composable simulation is new in the

---

[27] It is often claimed that models exist and should be assessed only for specific functions, such as making choices. That is not correct. In fact, one of the primary functions of models (including DoD's) is the recording, structuring, and communication of knowledge. Models capture and communicate our knowledge.

[28] Zeigler, Praehofer, and Kim, 2000.

history of DoD, the existing infrastructure is not always what one might like.

Implications. We assume that the better and more completely the science and technology of M&S are understood, and the more complete the tool kit embodying that technology, the more successful will be M&S composition efforts.

Research Issues. Are there degrees of quality of science and technology underlying M&S that would lead to predictions of likelihood of success in composability? If so, how can they be measured?[29] As part of this, how do we assess current and prospective policies and standards relevant to composability?

Understanding of Relevant Management Theory

Most DoD-related M&S composition efforts are large, no matter what size metric is being used: They involve multiple modules, they cross boundaries of "communities of interest," and they involve hundreds of people and perhaps hundreds or thousands of interface agreements and understandings to be negotiated. Effective performance of an M&S effort at this scale requires highly effective management. But is it more important for the project manager to be expert in M&S or in management techniques themselves (if one can't have both)? Are there, in fact, management techniques unique to, or tailored especially for, M&S development, especially M&S involving the composition of complex, preexisting modules? Certainly, the methods of software engineering and systems engineering are highly relevant, but are there special issues involved in large-scale composability efforts?

Many of the generic issues are familiar to systems engineers and technical managers. One we might mention is the need for strong

---

[29] A possible useful analogy is the Capability Maturity Models developed at the Software Engineering Institute, Carnegie Mellon University (see http://www.sei.cmu.edu/cmm/cmms/transition.html). These models provide a means of assessing the capability of an institution to develop quality software (within a specific domain of expertise) reliably and repeatably. A science of M&S might provide similar predictive power, based on the attributes of an organization, the tools being used, and the subject-matter domain within which modeling is being attempted.

architecture (of the substantive model itself, not just of low-level procedures). Where one finds a strong substantive-level architecture, it is usual to find a first-rate chief engineer, not just a number of committees. In the absence of this, "throwing people at the problem" may further increase the size of the project but not its probability of success, a point immortalized in *The Mythical Man Month,* which commented candidly on early IBM experience building complex operating systems (primarily System 360).[30] Although it is difficult to comment objectively here in the absence of documented histories and lessons-learned studies, it appears to us and to many of those with whom we discussed these matters that at least some large-scale DoD composability efforts have suffered from overly large and complicated programs that had shortfalls in design, coherence, and management.[31] An additional problem here is that even people trained well in traditional systems-engineering methods may not be well prepared for complex composition projects in which even reasonably good standards often prove insufficient and in which no clear-cut, top-down, detailed design is possible because of constant evolution. It appears that good practice currently requires frequent integrative experimentation and iteration, as well as a good but flexible design and good standards. This is particularly evident to those engaged in networked applications where the system is adapting to needs and capabilities.

Implications. We believe that effective management of a complex M&S project, especially one requiring composition of modules across communities of interest, is both an art and a science. If the management of such efforts were better understood and discussed, it

---

[30] See Brooks, 1995, which includes "Brooks's Law," i.e., that adding manpower to a late software project makes it later.

[31] One of the authors (Davis) recalls that in the course of a National Research Council study (see National Research Council, 1997a), many DoD model representatives were asked by panelists, "Who is your chief architect?" Often, the response was a blank expression or reference to some user committee. Sometimes, after a delay, the response was the name of a software-engineer contractor who was not, in fact, responsible for "substance." This experience underlay many of the concerns expressed in that document about the JWARS and JSIMS efforts, as of 1997.

is likely that successes traced to effective management could be replicated.

Research Issues. What are the management techniques that lead to successful M&S for complex projects involving composition of relatively complex and possibly evolving *models*, rather than just software components or simple models that merely provide services? How do we know? How can the relative contribution of management to project success be assessed? What can be done to acquaint managers with the knowledge they need? What can be done to improve the empirical base in this area?

Quality of Legacy M&S Modules, Framework, and Components

Since composition depends on having components, and since many—and perhaps most—DoD M&S components already exist, the legacy of those components is an important factor in determining the difficulty of composability. We shall not attempt to address the basic quality or validity of DoD component models here, other than to say that those models vary enormously and some are better candidates for reusable components than others. Reviewing such matters is far beyond the scope of the present effort.

One important aspect of the functional quality of legacy modules, however, is the documentation provided for them. Good documentation facilitates reuse and composability, because the characteristics and/or behavior of a module can be understood, even if that module is off the shelf and the original developers are not available. Some would argue that ideal documentation has all of those attributes and, in addition, is machine-interpretable—i.e., the documentation is metadata that can be the subject of search and the parameters of automatic or semi-automatic composition. Even far short of that alleged ideal, documentation is crucial—and typically poor.

Other aspects of quality for legacy modules involve clarity of architectural structure within the modules themselves, consistency of terminology, and well-conceived interfaces.

Implications. If the architecture and documentation of legacy models are poor or missing, it greatly increases the difficulty of composition. It may be vital for a module's developers to be accessible and perhaps even built into the composition team. That has implications for the size and composition of the development team, as well as the likely speed and effectiveness of development. Further, the resulting composition may itself be poorly architected and documented and difficult to comprehend, unless tidying up of legacy components is part of the development effort.

Research Issues. How can the quality of legacy modules be measured? What can and should be done when the architecture or documentation of components is poor? What standards should be adopted to avoid such problems in the future? What is the state of the art of creating metadata as documentation to represent the content and operation of a module?

As a here-and-now issue, if one considers a representative set of modules of interest to DoD, what is the actual state of their documentation? If it is poor, what steps (retrodocumentation) can be taken to make substantial improvements that would affect the ability to use these modules within larger compositions?

Strength of Human Considerations

People—and the knowledge and understanding they bring to the task—are essential for composability of models and simulations. Among the human considerations affecting success is the degree of shared "community" among the individuals; the quality of management available on the project; and the knowledge, experience, and skills of the project members who must design wrappers, interface agreements, networking connections, documentation, agents, objects, code, and all the other items that contribute to the success of a composition.

Common Community

By *community*, we mean a set of people sharing a common semantics and range of mutually understood contexts and tacit knowledge.[32] They need not be physically collocated, although that does help. Examples of communities relevant to M&S include Army logistics personnel, Air Force pilots, and electronic-warfare signals engineers. Note, however, that models are often composed across community boundaries, even if they are "owned" primarily by one community. For example, it is frequently desirable to plug a logistics or weather model into a given "primary" model, precisely because the community creating or using the given model may not possess the relevant expertise to model those other aspects. Composed models are often likely to bridge communities, implying that semantics will be a problem.

Like most of the other dimensions, community is a spectrum. At its simplest, all the modules from which a composition is to be made have been constructed by members of the same community, and members of that community are themselves performing the composition. At its most complex, modules come from different communities and therefore do not have a shared semantics within their differing internal operations or in the interface they present. There are, of course, many intermediate points in this community spectrum where some concepts and terminology are shared and others are not.

Implications. We believe this dimension might be the single most predictive indicator of composability success or failure.[33] In

---

[32] Linguists often distinguish among syntax, semantics, and pragmatics, with the latter referring to the context-dependence of semantics. For our purposes, we use *common semantics* or *shared semantics* as a blanket term covering all of these aspects of language. On the other hand, we have sought to highlight *in-context validity* as another key factor because *semantics* is usually thought of by those engaged in M&S simply as *meaning*, without regard to validity.

[33] In stressing the significance of community, or preferably of a close-knit group (whether or not collocated physically), we have been influenced by our own experiences in development of the RAND Strategy Assessment System (RSAS), the experiences of RAND colleagues Randall Steeb and John Matsumura (see Appendix E), and the commercial-world experience of Steven Hall of Lockheed-Martin (see Appendix E). These were all *analytic* efforts requiring rigor, but they included a good deal of modular activity and composition.

composability projects of substantial size, if interface "contracts" must be hammered out among differing parties not sharing a robust semantics and similar tacit knowledge, there will be misunderstandings, and it will take considerable time or even prove just too hard, with the project failing altogether.

Research Issues. How can the degree of community cohesion or uniformity be measured among parties to a composability project? Are there means of quickly increasing the degree of community among disparate groups and individuals when that is needed for a project?

Quality of Management

Science-and-technology-related knowledge, discussed above, involves the science and technology of management: How much is known about the effective management of complex M&S projects? This factor deals with a project's management itself: How well does it apply whatever is known about successful M&S management? Is a particular person trained in M&S management? Has he or she read the relevant texts? Does he or she have relevant prior experience?

Implications. In our experience, management matters a lot. Too often, it appears that someone is put in charge of a complex DoD M&S effort who knows little about M&S technology or the subject matter being modeled. In the case of uniformed officers, they also tend to be on the job for only a short time relative to the multiyear time frame required for an M&S effort to be started, performed, accomplished, and assessed. This situation most likely has very deleterious effects, but at present we have no way of measuring such effects other than obtaining anecdotal evidence. Finally, we note again that even some exposure to systems engineering is not enough, because—currently, at least—systems engineers are often not trained to think about *model* composition, as distinct from composition of software components. They are too exclusively focused on interfaces, which are ultimately the simple part of model composability. They may also be exposed primarily to static systems, for which evolution is a non-problem.

Research Issues. What education, training, and experience are necessary for someone leading a complex M&S effort, especially one involving composition of modules? How can the quality of management be assessed? Is it possible to trace the success, or failure, of complex M&S efforts to effective, or ineffective, management?

Quality of the Human Capital That Builds M&S

Composition of models or simulations is a process performed by people on a project team. Those people bring certain knowledge and skills to the task that can greatly affect the success of the effort. They need to be able to understand the structure and operation of existing modules to be composed; they must understand those modules' interfaces and the contracts that must be negotiated to allow data transfers among those modules; they often must develop wrappers or other software "Band-Aids" to interface incompatible modules with one another. And they must be able to work cooperatively as a team, knowing when there are misunderstandings about or misinterpretations of terminology, concepts, and technology.

Implications. The quality of the members of the project team is one of the most direct, relevant factors determining the likelihood of success of a venture.

Research Issues. How do we assess the relevance and quality of persons assembled to perform a complex M&S composition or development project? What education, experience, and training should all project participants have? Do DoD contracting policies reward hiring top talent or lowest-cost programmers?

Some Issues Regarding the Above Factors

We have characterized the above dimensions as a first cut at a systematic way of understanding what makes composability more or less difficult. We have no illusions about the list being complete, although it reflects some months of research and discussion with people in the M&S community. Our factors are a beginning, not an end. To emphasize this point, we highlight here some research issues raised by our categorization:

- *Which factors are missing?* What characteristics of modules or the composability process that affect a successful outcome have not been captured by the above dimensions?
- *Which factors are not expected to have a meaningful impact* on the success of composability and might therefore be pruned from the list?
- *Do the factors cluster into larger, more meaningful, more practical categories?* The listed factors are often difficult to measure and interpret. Are there fewer, simpler categories that cluster several of these dimensions or that better represent typical model or simulation construction and assemblage processes? If so, what are they?

As one example of a missing factor, we admit to not having discussed issues such as the existence of a marketplace for components, which might create competition and improve quality while lowering costs. This is an important issue, but it is simply not addressed here. Some software experts regard market issues as fundamental to the concept of component-based development (e.g., Szyperski, 2002) and point to numerous commercial developments that use this approach. Regrettably, it appeared to us that DoD's M&S composability efforts are not obviously at a stage of maturity where these matters could be discussed meaningfully.

Another mostly missing subject is simulation-based acquisition (SBA), which has enormous potential, commercially as well as in DoD M&S applications. We have largely omitted it because it is only one of several application-area subjects, along with various types of training and doctrine development, operations planning, and so on, and because a good deal of material has already been published on the subject. Major parts of the related vision are slowly becoming a reality in industry. Appendix F provides some relevant highlights and citations.

CHAPTER THREE

Recommendations

Using a Systems Approach

In the previous chapters we have sought to establish a framework for diagnosing issues, a number of which we have identified. Although the questions are many, in this chapter we turn our attention to preliminary prescriptions. Where should DoD go from here if it wishes to improve composability?

A framework is needed to accomplish the convergence. The framework we use is shown in Figure 3.1, which suggests targets for action. The concept underlying Figure 3.1 is that the DMSO's investments and priorities can improve the science and technology base for composability, on which all else depends. Since science and technology are a bit diffuse, however, we see a need for pulling together the "understanding," or "appreciation," of the composability problem. In particular, people—especially users or consumers of M&S-based work—should understand the kinds of distinctions we discuss in Chapter Two and should have a good sense of what level of composability ambitiousness is appropriate for their application and what limits or red flags they should see. Having science, technology, and understanding is not enough, however. Large model-building efforts will frequently fail—as they have in recent years—because of a combination of ineffectual management and highly varied quality and background in the workforce. DoD investments could, over time, improve both management and the quality of the simulation workforce. Finally, there is the matter of ending up with a vital and

Figure 3.1
Targets of a Systems Approach to Improving Composability

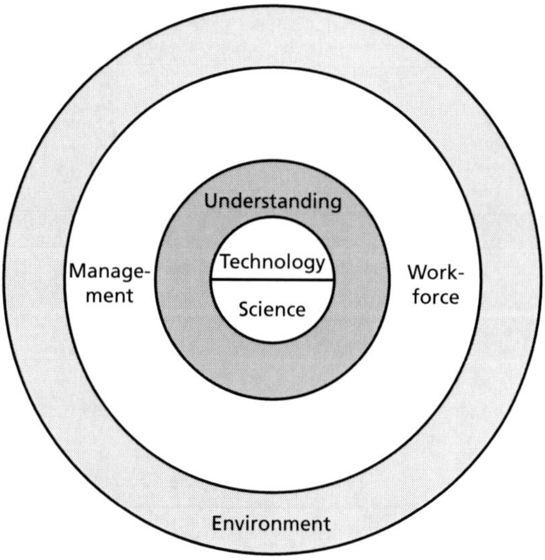

RAND *MG101-S.3-A*

dynamic overall environment for composability-related DoD M&S. That will depend not only on the internal elements, but also on industry having the proper incentives and the existence of a mix of stable centers of excellence and dynamic competition. By analogy with other DoD endeavors, we would expect an important part of that infrastructure to be well-lubricated connections with commercial industry.[1]

We also believe that in planning for improvements in composability, DoD should think primarily in terms of leveraging commercial and academic developments, rather than "doing its own thing." Figure 3.2 suggests notionally that DoD should merely watch developments that are not particularly important to its own needs (left

---

[1] Our framework has a fair amount in common with a process-engineering approach suggested at a recent meeting on improving data practices (see Appendix C). That approach emphasizes that organizations are made up of people, who operate within organizations and cultures. In our view, the best way to change cultural behavior is to change objective realities and incentives in sound ways.

Figure 3.2
Leveraging Versus Unique Investments

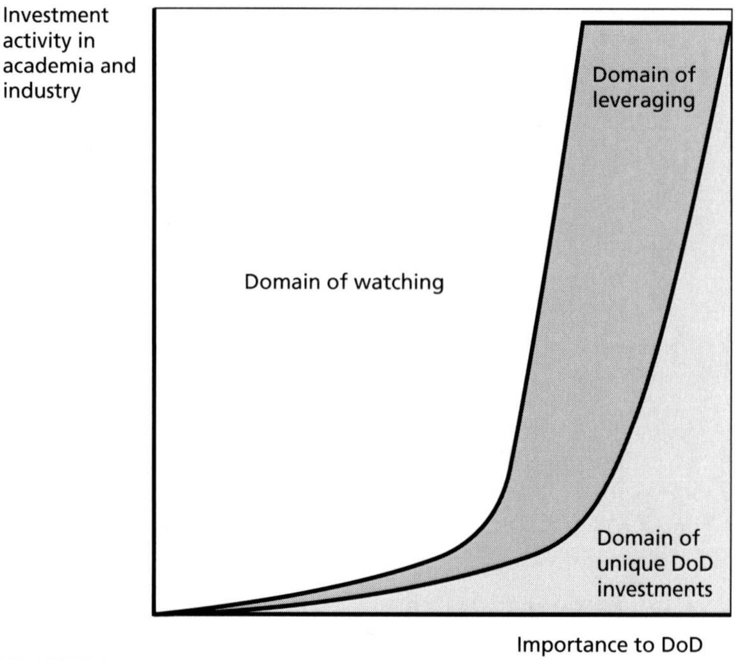

RAND *MG101-3.2*

side), that it should invest with the notion of greatly leveraging others' investments where there are DoD applications that can make use of general trends (domain of leveraging), and that it should make more unique investments only where the stakes are very high and the necessary technological developments are not occurring elsewhere (domain of unique DoD investments).

We shall return to this perspective at the end of the chapter.

With this background, let us now move to conclusions and recommendations based on the structure in Figure 3.1.

Science

A limiting factor for progress on composability is the state of relevant science. We distinguish here between the science of the substantive subject areas being modeled and the science of relevant modeling and simulation.

Science of the Subjects Being Modeled

Few would claim that existing models represent past warfare accurately in all respects, much less that they permit reliable prediction. However difficult the past problems have been, the difficulties have increased because we are now in an era of rapid military change. Some of the new issues for which the relevant military science needs to be developed include

- Effects-based planning, with its emphasis on affecting *behaviors* of individuals, military units, and larger elements of society, as well as its effort to depict and deal with military operations within the paradigm of complex adaptive systems.[2]
- Network-centric operations.[3]
- An unprecedented degree of jointness, sometimes down to the tactical or engagement levels[4] (e.g., close coupling between special forces and general-purpose forces, as when the former provide target spotting for precision fires).
- Operational- and tactical-level maneuver doctrine suitable for an era of extremely lethal and accurate weapons.[5]

---

[2] See Deptula, 2001; Smith, 2003; and Davis, 2001a.

[3] See Alberts, Garstka, and Stein, 1999; National Research Council, 2000.

[4] For a discussion of this and other command-and-control issues, see Alberts, Garstka, Hayes, and Signori, 2001.

[5] See, e.g., Clark, 2002, for a discussion of operational maneuver from the sea. See Army Science Board, 2001, for a discussion of Army concepts emphasizing airlift; and Gritton, Davis, Steeb, and Matsumura, 2000, for a discussion downplaying the role of air mobility, except for leading-edge Army forces, in favor of sealift, especially prepositioned assets.

- Increasing use of unmanned platforms for most aspects of C4ISR and even weapon delivery (e.g., unmanned aerial vehicles (UAVs), unmanned combat aerial vehicles (UCAVs), battlefield robots, nanotechnology "insect-like" surveillance,[6] and defense systems with modes of automated fire).

Even this short list should convey a sense of how much new, in-depth thinking will be necessary. That thinking, of course, will have to be translated into sound models and simulations, the quality of which will depend on the quality of the underlying military science.[7] A laudable example of a DoD effort to establish foundations for new military science is the work of the Command and Control Research Program (CCRP) within the Office of the Secretary of Defense (see http://www.dodccrp.org). This effort has brought together a community of people and encouraged serious discussion and publication of ideas, although not typically at a high level of rigor.

The new U.S. Joint Forces Command (USJFCOM) may be a natural focal point for much of the new thinking, but it remains to be seen whether it will see a role for itself in developing and documenting definitive information. So far, it has focused on joint experimentation, but not on creating a solid and enduring knowledge base.[8]

More generally, our recommendation here is that

- **DMSO should work with the services and other DoD agencies (including USJFCOM) to identify key warfare areas for which the relevant military science needs to be developed and codified. DMSO should then advocate support of related applied research programs.**

---

[6] National Academy of Sciences, 2003.

[7] This was discussed at length in National Research Council, 1997a, at a time when a great deal was being invested in modeling and simulation software, but there was relatively little fresh thinking about content.

[8] See Davis, 2002b, for discussion. A similar theme is emphasized in a forthcoming National Research Council report on a study conducted for the Department of the Navy addressing its approach to experimentation.

The various existing focus areas used in official documents may or may not be the proper focus areas for assuring development of the appropriate military science: Sometimes the natural categories for systematic inquiry are not the same as those identified by authors of documents such as the Joint Vision series and the Quadrennial Defense Review. Still, we note that DMSO's current technology thrusts—C4I to Sim, dynamic environment, human performance, and knowledge integration—all include related activities.[9]

Another suggestion that has been repeatedly made in very recent years is that (in our words) the military science of DoD M&S and C4ISR should be increasingly integrated.[10] Historically, the M&S and C4ISR worlds have proceeded rather independently, even though there should be a great deal of commonality, as suggested by Figure 3.3. The figure lays out the scope of issues being considered under C4ISR; in the center are many for which M&S would be relevant, and around the edges are many others to which it should connect well.

Key decisions within command and control, for example, should logically be supported by M&S activities exploring alternative courses of action; and the inputs and outputs of M&S should be conceived so as to relate well to the elements of the common operational picture being pursued vigorously in the realm of command and control. Many examples could be given. We conclude that

- **DMSO should investigate how best to bring about a convergence of activities, where appropriate, in the M&S and command-and-control domains.**

---

[9] See www.dmso.mil/public.

[10] See Tolk, 2003, and Tolk and Hieb, 2003. We thank Andreas Tolk for providing the latter report prior to publication. Figure 3.3 was used in a NATO C4ISR code-of-best-practices manual, issued in 2000, which is quite germane to model composability (we have not yet had the opportunity to read it).

Figure 3.3
Functions of C4ISR for the Warfighter

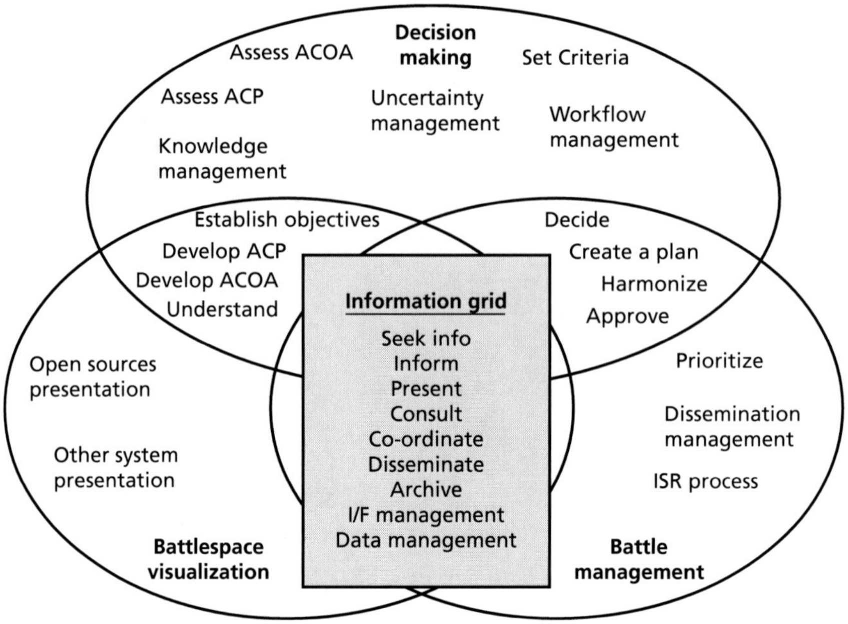

SOURCE: Tolk and Hieb, 2003.
RAND *MG101-3.3*

Science of Modeling and Simulation

Assuming that the substance of the phenomena being modeled is understood, the issue then becomes how that knowledge is represented in models and simulations. Many of the foundations have in fact been laid. Regrettably, most of the M&S community appears not yet to be familiar with those foundations, which it often regards as "too theoretical," perhaps because the practitioners did not study them during their university years or perhaps because many of them prefer to just "do" modeling and simulation rather than understand the underlying concepts and methods. Significantly, we do not believe that most of the existing texts are suitably tailored for the managers and workforce of DoD M&S. We discuss the issue later in this chapter.[11]

Even though M&S is now a relatively mature subject in some respects, the ability to develop composable systems describing modern military operations will depend on advances on many fronts. Among the cutting-edge issues here are

- Rigorous language for describing models, simulations, and many of the subtleties therein.[12]
- Representations suitable to effective communication and transfer and to the composition of models that have been developed in different formalisms or representations.[13]
- Model abstraction and the related subjects of aggregation and disaggregation. Multiresolution, multiperspective modeling (MRMPM) is an enabler for composability efforts that assemble components vertically.[14]
- Development of effective "heterogeneous" simulations, by which we mean simulations that combine components with very different formalisms and representations.[15]

---

[11] An exception, although it covers only some of the needed material, is Cloud and Rainey, 1998, a collected volume assembled in a coherent way by the U.S. Air Force Academy. It includes chapters on both foundational theory and practice, drawing upon the knowledge of many authors with considerable hands-on experience. It also contains numerous references to the literature.

[12] See Petty and Weisel, 2003, for an excellent set of composability-related definitions and related discussion. See also the textbook by Zeigler, Praehofer, and Kim, 2000.

[13] See the report of the working group on grand challenges in modeling and simulation methods in Fujimoto et al., 2002, for discussion of grand challenges in the areas of abstraction, formalism, and multimodeling (http://www.informatik.uni-rostock.de/~lin/GC/report/Methods.html). Contributors include Paul Davis, Paul Fishwick, and Hans Vangheluwe, among others.

[14] For one stream of research, see Davis and Bigelow, 1998; Davis and Bigelow, 2003; and Bigelow and Davis, 2003. For related work on hierarchical decompositions done by the U.S. Army, see Deitz, Harris, Bray, Sheehan, Wong, and Purdy, 2003; and Nelson, 2003. This work ties decompositions to realistic operations and universal task lists.

[15] Some of these issues have been discussed extensively by Paul Fishwick (see Fujimoto et al., 2002; and Fishwick, 1995, an earlier text that refers to "multimodeling").

- Formalisms for specifying the syntax of discrete, continuous, and hybrid simulation models unambiguously.
- Explanation mechanisms, including the agent-based models and simulations[16] that are becoming extremely important but tend to be difficult to use analytically because understanding cause and effect is complicated by adaptive behaviors of the agents.[17,18]
- Man-machine interactions as increasingly sophisticated human behaviors are being built into "avatars" in virtual-reality simulations. These are likely to become extremely important in future training applications, and present-day world commercial games, including a few DoD-specialized games, already provide strong images of what the future may hold. Assuring that the methods and science keep up with the technology here is a major challenge.[19]
- Methods for routinely increasing the shelf life of components, probably through parameterization.

Elaboration on Specification

With respect to specification issues, a challenge crying out for communitywide convergence is the need to combine formalisms such as

---

[16] See Fujimoto et al., 2002, for a report from a workshop. Speakers' initial PowerPoint presentations, as well as working-group presentations in briefing form, are listed there under "Workshop Programme." Short text summaries of working group reports appear separately. The overall report is available in PDF format.

[17] See Uhrmacher, Fishwick, and Zeigler, 2001, for a review of agent-based modeling issues. See also the grand-challenges discussion in Fujimoto et al., 2002.

[18] We thank colleagues Randall Steeb and John Matsumura for sharing their decade-long experience with composition and for emphasizing that they see explanation capabilities as fundamentally limiting.

[19] See, e.g., Uhrmacher and Swartout, 2003, which includes a discussion by William Swartout of work at the University of Southern California on Army-sponsored virtual-reality simulation for mission rehearsal. Many of the related challenges involve artificial-intelligence representation of human behaviors ranging from decisions to facial expressions and gesturing.

the unified modeling language (UML) or its variants,[20] which are best suited for syntactic matters, with formalisms specific to simulation, which are important for specifying subtleties such as time-management issues, e.g., when the phenomena being modeled involve a mix of continuous and discrete events

Figure 3.4 depicts such a composite approach. In the UML world, use-cases, class diagrams, state diagrams, and the like facilitate modern object-oriented design and establish a good foundation. However, they are not currently sufficiently expressive to fully specify models for simulation, which often involve complex and subtle time-ordering issues, a simple example of which is illustrated in Appendix D. The shortcomings can be addressed with systems concepts such as the concept of behavior (sets of input/output pairs of time-based functions), components, their couplings, and test cases.[21] Relevant methods include discrete event system specifications (DEVS), Petri nets, and Bond graphs.

We see the UML designs as providing a good but incomplete top-down view, whereas a systems formalism provides a more comprehensive, bottom-up view, which is especially important for designing component-level modules intended to fit together coherently in various simulations. As discussed in Appendix E, Lockheed-Martin's Space Division has used DEVS methodology[22] for a modular (composable) approach to M&S that has been used on about a

---

[20] The definitive resources for UML can be found at a website of the Rational Software Corporation (see http://www.rational.com/uml/resources/documentation/index.jspA). For a single readable source, see Albir, 1998.

[21] See, e.g., Zeigler, Praehofer, and Kim, 2000; and Zeigler and Sarjoughian, 2002. Figure 3.4 is adapted from a private communication, based on current systems-engineering lectures (Zeigler, 2003).

[22] One function that the DEVS formalism serves is that of describing the "operating system" for simulation. That is, at run time, the simulator has to assure that events occur in proper order and that inputs and outputs flow to the appropriate components. This function of DEVS has been referred to in "virtual machine" terms by McGill University professor Hans Vansgheluwe (http://moncs.cs.mcgill.ca/MSDL/).

Figure 3.4
Relationships Between UML and Systems Concepts

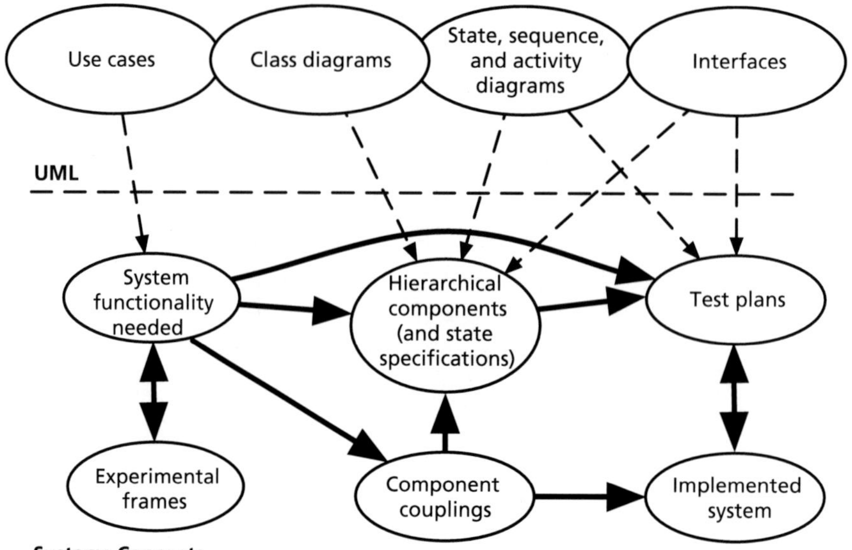

RAND *MG101-3.4*

dozen major components (e.g., for a radar sensor) in a dozen or so different applications in which appropriate components were composed for assessing systems concepts. Composing a particular simulation for a particular application has typically taken weeks to months, depending on the extent of new modeling necessary, with only days or a few weeks necessary for the part of the composition involving preexisting modules.[23]

Elaboration on Families of Models and Games

Another class of issues arises when one focuses on the fact that modeling and simulation is not usually done for its own sake, but rather to support applications, such as analysis for any of a number of purposes, including weapon-system acquisition, interpretation of experiments, and doctrinal assessment. Ideally, M&S should be con-

[23] Personal communication, Steve Hall, Lockheed-Martin Space Division.

structed so as to serve these applications well. A key element of this issue is increasingly recognized to be the need in many instances for work groups to have *families* of models and games.[24] The family concept recognizes the need to work at both different resolutions and in different perspectives. Including games in the family is important because, in practice, much of the most innovative work requires human involvement. One of the "dirty little secrets" of DoD's M&S work is that forward-looking warfighters have often ignored M&S-based work while using old-fashioned tabletop games to conceive and think about new concepts. That practice, however, has sometimes led to serious problems, as when a service's concept developers take liberties with the laws of physics and reasonable extrapolations of technological capability.

Relating this to the subject of composability, it should be possible to go from human-intensive concepts work, to the development or adaptation of modules representing the concept well, to the incorporation of those modules in simulations. The imagery would be one of, "Ah, now I see what you're talking about. Work up the necessary model modifications and we will incorporate them in [the comprehensive model of choice] for serious analysis," followed by module development and adaptation, and by plug-and-play. Making this a reality in an efficient workplace, however, is a cutting-edge challenge except within narrow domains.

Another "dirty little secret" has been that high-level planners —in industry as well as DoD—often resort either to unaided intuitive analysis or to simple models bearing no clear-cut relationship to the more detailed models and simulations in which large sums of money have been invested. A core reason for this has been the fact that higher-level planners require synoptic views and must deal with massive uncertainty, neither of which are treated well by the more

---

[24] This is discussed briefly in Davis, 2002a, and illustrated in more detail in Davis, Bigelow, and McEver, 2001. A number of organizations have had model families over the years. The U.S. Air Force, for example, has long worked with a set of models ranging from one at the level of individual air-to-air engagements (Brawler) to one describing theater-level combat (Thunder).

detailed M&S. The Department of Defense has recently decided to move formally and practically to *capabilities-based planning* (see Rumsfeld, 2001), which poses great related demands. The enablers for this type of planning include MRMPM and the related families of models and games, as well as the relatively new concept of *exploratory analysis* (see Davis, 2002a). That, in turn, poses deep issues about fundamentals such as what constitutes model "validation." How can a model or simulation be considered "valid," even if it is the best example available and considered to be useful, when either the model itself or the data on which it relies are highly uncertain?[25]

Opportunities

Although much remains to be done in the science of M&S, the subject appears to be ripe for synthesis and convergence on at least a substantial starter set of fundamentals and best practices. We recommend that

- **DMSO should commission development of a primer on the science of military-relevant M&S: what can be done, issues, factors, key references, and best practices. This would cover issues such as model abstraction, model families, and model composability.**
- **DMSO should also support empirical studies of success and failure in composability efforts, in order to provide something better than anecdotal knowledge on the matter. These studies should identify metrics that can be usefully applied in understanding the difficulties associated with different composability efforts.**

---

[25] The general issue of model verification and validation was treated at length in the New Foundations workshop documented on the DMSO website (https://www.dmso.mil/public/transition/vva/foundations). One report stimulated by that meeting recommends generalizing the concept of validation to make it realistic for exploratory analysis (Bigelow and Davis, 2003). For a good overview of verification, validation, and accreditation of simulation models, see Pace, 2003.

The primer development could be seen as a two-year effort. Although analogies are always imperfect, DMSO's work on verification, validation, and accreditation is to some extent a model. That work drew on a broad community, was focused on being ultimately useful, and led to a substantial knowledge base, much of it pointing to relevant existing literature. DMSO has also seen this appropriately as a living subject and has continued to sponsor a related technical working group and scientific conferences.[26]

Fortunately, many past and current activities could be drawn upon in this effort. Scientific and technical communities already exist;[27] some relevant textbooks already exist;[28] and some groundwork has been laid.[29]

Technology

Methods and Tools

It is often difficult to distinguish between challenges and developments in technology rather than science. Furthermore, it is not as though science leads technology, as one might expect from a certain philosophical view. Science often lags technological developments substantially. Engineers and other "builders" learn how to do things that are exciting, useful, or both, and it may take years for these developments to be integrated into a set of principles that could be

[26] See https://www.dmso.mil/public/transition/vva/foundations.

[27] Examples here include the Software Integration Standards Organization and the Society for Computer Simulation.

[28] See, e.g., Zeigler, Praehofer, and Kim, 2000; Singhal and Zyda, 1999; and Law and Kelton, 1991, among others. Cloud and Rainey, 1998, covers well a number of subjects of interest to DoD. The National Academies have also published very useful reference documents such as National Research Council, 1997a; National Research Council, 1997b; and National Research Council, 2002.

[29] The Army Modeling and Simulation Office and DMSO co-sponsored a simulation-science workshop in 2002, the report from which is available on-line (Harmon, 2002).

called science. The following are examples of key technological issues in military-relevant M&S technology:

- Tools and environments to facilitate development of complex, composable simulations (perhaps by analogy to the common environment used extensively in C4ISR) (see Carr and Myers, 2003; and Tolk, 2003).
- Man-machine pools to assist in model abstraction and its converse (i.e., in model aggregation and disaggregation). These should include tools for at-the-time "smart" metamodeling (repro modeling) that combines approximate structural knowledge for the particular subject area with statistical methods that can be largely automated.[30] It should be possible to apply the tools locally, within a larger model, as well as to complete models or major components.[31]
- Developing "mapping machines" to help translate simulation components from one representation or formalism to another that is more suitable for a given simulation application. Figure 3.5 suggests an image developed in a recent international workshop.[32] This image envisions taking a range of data and expressions of needs and tailoring a set of mutually informed and calibrated multiresolution, multiperspective models for that context.
- New methods and man-machine tools for model documentation and, equally important, for effective communication of concepts from one group of modelers to another. These might look less like traditional hardcopy volumes, or even today's online help files, than like a kind of virtual reality akin to that used by chemists recording, studying, and communicating the

[30] See Davis and Bigelow, 2003.

[31] One modest example of this is given in Davis, 2001b.

[32] See Fujimoto et al., 2002, particularly the paper by Vanghueluwe and Mosterman (http://www.informatik.uni-rostock.de/~lin/GC/Slides/Vangheluwe.pdf) and the report of the modeling and simulation methods group (http://www.informatik.uni-rostock.de/~lin/GC/report/Methods.html). Figure 3.5 is adapted from a figure in that report.

Figure 3.5
Building Capabilities for Creating, Transforming, and Tailoring MRMPM

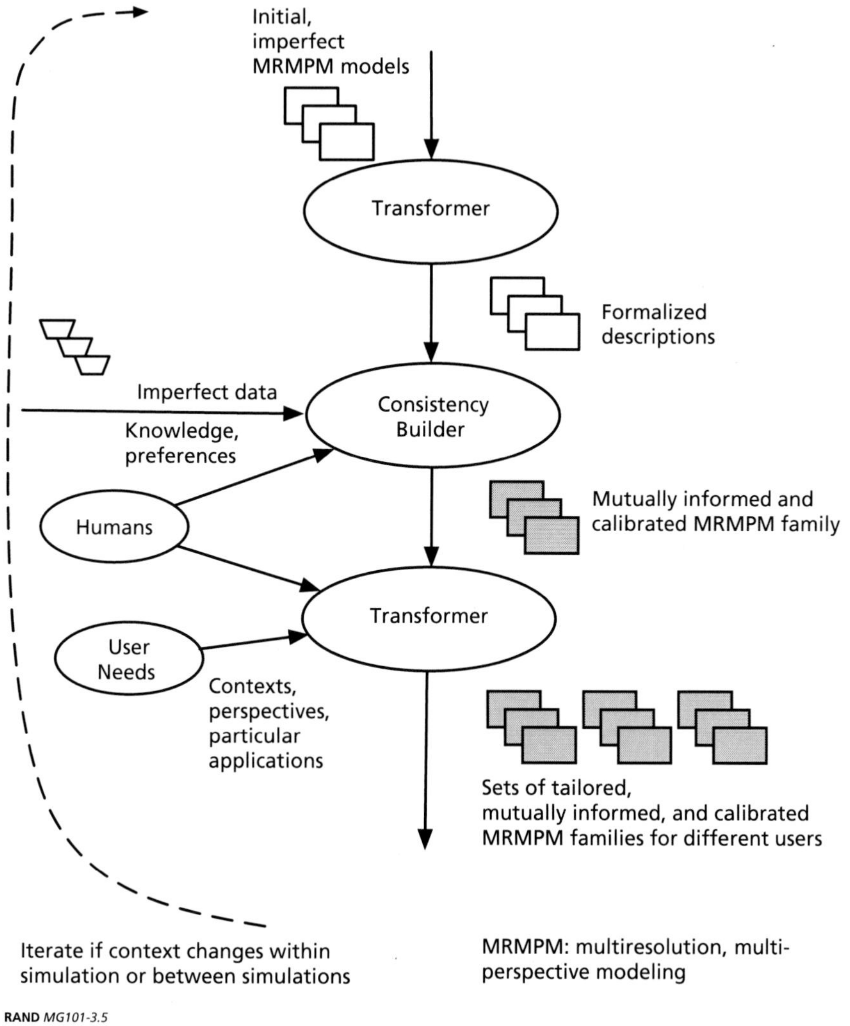

RAND *MG101-3.5*

structure of complex organic molecules. Or they might mimic the ways in which people learn rules by participating in entertainment games (or war games).

We recommend that

- **DMSO should have or should advocate research programs in the above areas.**

Standards

A historically central role for DMSO has been development, championing, and enforcement of standards for M&S. Standards are almost always controversial and can either be constructive and enabling or seriously counterproductive. However controversial they may be, however, some standards are essential in activities such as assuring the future interoperability of U.S. military forces or assuring reasonable degrees of composability in DoD-sponsored military simulations. The issue is not whether, but which. DoD's decree that all DoD M&S would be written in Ada has become a classic example of a dubious decision. In contrast, most observers of and participants in DoD-related M&S agree that development of the high-level architecture (HLA) and its implementation in the run-time infrastructure (RTI) were important and constructive events that helped enable rapid progress in distributed training and exercises.

This said, an important question is, What next?, particularly as it relates to composability. The best standards often emerge bottom-up as the result of practitioners seeing firsthand what is really needed. It seems to us that the time is ripe for deciding on the next phase of standards.

One discussion of the HLA's limitations (Singhal and Zyda, 1999, p. 282), states

> However, the HLA does not go all the way toward supporting dynamically composable simulations and universal reuse. Federation development is static, meaning that the object model and information exchanges must be completed before the simu-

> lation run begins. At runtime, federates may enter and leave the simulation at will, but only as long as they conform to the predefined object model being used by that simulation. Thus, reuse is limited to HLA systems associated with compatible object models. An HLA system, once specified, cannot support the runtime introduction of arbitrary federates and, therefore, cannot fully exploit dynamic composability.

Many other suggestions have been made in recent years about ways to extend or adapt HLA/RTI methods. Some of the suggestions call for what amounts to incremental evolution of the HLA/RTI, with occasional bending of the rules as a bow to necessity.[33] Others (see Tolk, 2002; Tolk, 2003; and Tolk and Hieb, 2003) call for a more dramatic reworking of DoD standards to be better aligned with the momentum of the commercial sector, which is bursting with activity associated with the model driven architecture (MDA), XML and XMI,[34] web services, and so on.[35] Much of what has been accomplished by the MOVES Institute at the Naval Postgraduate School would not have been possible but for such developments, in which the Institute is very active.[36] It is our understanding[37] that XMSF aspires to replace not only the RTI layer of HLA, but also the higher-level negotiations of HLA itself, while at the same time increasing support for dynamically composable simulations. We conclude that

---

[33] The recent Millennium Challenge 2002 experiment by the U.S. Joint Forces Command was an impressive success of composability for limited purposes (the resulting federation was a temporary artifact that supported the exercise and related experimentation), but it was accomplished only with great difficulty and at great expense, some of which was caused by the rigidity of the HLA/RTI protocols. Compromises were eventually struck, but considerable frustration arose along the way. An account of the federation building is given in Ceranowicz, Torpey, Helfinstine, Evans, and Hines, 2002.

[34] Some of these are discussed briefly in Appendix C.

[35] Many related developments are discussed in depth in Szyperski, 2002.

[36] The Institute's website is http://www.movesinstitute.org/. One Institute product is the now-famous "Army Game."

[37] Personal communication, Don Brutzman, Naval Postgraduate School.

- **DMSO should move quickly to have a soul-searching review of what next-generation standards should be and about how best to assure effective connections with commercial developments. Extensions of HLA/RTI should allow for dynamic composability, but it may be that this would be only part of a larger shift to a web-services framework such as that of the XMSF project. Such a review could be analogous to the one in the early 1990s that preceded development of the HLA.**
- **Separately, DMSO should develop and promulgate standards to assure high-level documentation of M&S components and databases. It should commission a study to recommend such standards within perhaps one to two years. The terms of reference might specifically mention the possibility of combining UML and XML methods and of supplementing them with methods necessary to define rigorously the treatment of time in simulation.**

For a discussion of what UML and XML methods accomplish and how more is needed in dealing with the "simulation layer" and the treatment of time, see Zeigler, 2003, or Zeigler and Sarjoughian, 2002. The former is nonmathematical and has a good worked-out example.

Understanding

Improving the base of science and technology is not necessarily enough in itself. Success in composable simulation activities will also require that the relevant knowledge be synthesized, codified, and taught. There is a need to have living "bibles" for ubiquitous use in the community: primers of different types serving the needs of researchers, systems analysts, and managers; and one or more authoritative peer-reviewed journals to provide up-to-date *syntheses* of state-of-the-art knowledge and practice (i.e., reviews and definitive articles, rather than conference presentations).

In addition, it seems to us that understanding will be signaled by the emergence of useful metrics to help those engaged in M&S to better understand what they are getting into, what is more and less feasible, and how to improve odds of success and reduce risks. We recommend the following:

- **DMSO should sponsor research for the purpose of developing and testing metrics to characterize feasibility, risk, and cost of M&S efforts differing along the dimensions we have sketched (in Chapter Two) and others that may be suggested.**
- **The approach should be hierarchical, providing metrics by class of issue (e.g., the four categories in Chapter Two), the subcomponents thereof, and rollups of different types.**
- **The approach should also distinguish among levels of composability (e.g., atomic behaviors versus large-scale federations).**

We cannot predict now how well this research would go, but there is a clear need for methods by which to measure (both quantitatively and qualitatively) composability accomplishments or proposals. An analogy here is to technological-maturity assessments.

An important aspect of developing this level of understanding will be educating clients to better appreciate what can and cannot currently be accomplished, and at what price and with what risks.

Management

It is widely believed that one of the principal sources of failure or disappointment in past DoD composability efforts has been management itself. This, of course, is a sensitive subject. Nonetheless, the following criticisms frequently arise anecdotally:

There was no chief architect, or even recognition that a chief architect was needed.[38] To the extent that there was a de facto chief architect, it was sometimes a committee and sometimes someone not particularly brilliant.

The program managers were simply not educated adequately for such a technologically demanding job. They even lacked background in modeling, simulation, and analysis, much less background in that plus the particular management skills needed to build a complex modular system.[39]

To make things worse, interservice politics intruded. The name of the game, as seen by managers, has often been to "make sure all the services are happy," which may have little or nothing to do with creating a good and coherent system of systems. This problem, of course, is related to the larger issues of jointness.

Related to the above items, no one ever did a good job of picking out the stars and giving them support while killing off the underperformers.

Efforts were episodic, fragmented, and sometimes underfunded. Top talent in the individual companies would often do first-rate creative work but would then be moved elsewhere as new competitions emerged, current-project funding dried up temporarily, etc.

There was no real discipline of the sort one would see at a prime contractor in industry, where the resulting product must actually perform and prove reliable.

---

[38] This problem was cited as early as 1996 in a study by the Naval Studies Board, which was reviewing the state of modeling and simulation (National Research Council, 1997a).

[39] Secretary of the Air Force James Roche and Secretary of the Navy Gordon England have instituted a cooperative arrangement between the Air Force Institute of Technology and the Navy Postgraduate School (NPS) that will allow a much larger number of officers to be accommodated in military-relevant advanced education. Roche has directed that the number of Air Force students enrolled annually in graduate education be increased from 500 to 2,500 by fiscal 2009.

To this we would add our own observation, mirroring the comments of many colleagues in the community as well:

> Composability efforts have suffered from the fact that, while systems engineering talents are essential, they are currently inadequate because systems engineering typically views models as mere black boxes with interfaces, whereas the real difficulties of model composition involve substantive matters that often require a fairly deep understanding of the black boxes and the contexts in which the components are and are not suitable.

Against this background, we recommend the following:

- **DMSO should call for a special study, in cooperation with the services, the Joint Staff, and other agencies such as the Defense Management School, to define actions to be taken to improve the preparation of senior military officers and civilians who will occupy leadership positions in modeling and simulation.**
- **The terms of reference should emphasize the need for follow-up action by specifically calling out a number of candidate actions. These should include**
  - Reviewing the credentialing requirements for candidates, placing greater emphasis on strong and relevant technical background.
  - Development of n-week "at-the-time" preparation courses that appointees would take before assuming their new positions.
  - As part of the preparation-course effort, develop a primer that is management-oriented, drawing upon best practices in both government and industry.
  - Review time-in-place practices for military officers.
  - Develop partnerships with top-tier universities that have track records in large and complex composability-related work.
  - Develop measures of performance related to the quality of the workforce employed in projects and, of course, to results ob-

tained. Consider building in a lag time so that successes or failures that occur after rotation but because of actions taken on the assignment in question will affect later performance evaluations.

- **One goal of this study should be to suggest enhancements of the curricula for those studying systems engineering to better equip them for dealing with the substance of model composition.**

Quality of the Workforce

Many concerns have been expressed about inconsistencies in the workforce of those actually building simulations. A problem here is that simulation has traditionally been a technique that people pick up after having been educated in engineering, computer science, science, or other fields. Simulation, however, has many subtleties, and building large-scale composable simulations requires more than what one can easily "pick up" by doing. Particular areas of difficulty include (1) managing simulated time and events, (2) conceptual modeling, (3) abstraction and representation, and (4) measuring correspondence between simulation and target system.[40]

Some progress has been made on the related issue of certification programs. For example, Rogers, Amico, and Yerkes, 2002, describes a professional certification program under the auspices of the National Training Systems Association. See also the website of the Modeling and Simulation Professional Certification Commission (M&SPCC), http://www.simprofessional.org/about/who.html.[41]

---

[40] See Harmon, 2002, for a lengthy discussion. Del Lunceford, of the Army Modeling and Simulation Office, has recommended a degree program for simulation professionals, a set of best practices, and a set of processes to support those practices. In addition, he has spoken of needing a set of courses to install best practices (see Session 6 of the workshop discussed in Harmon, 2002).

[41] Some academic programs in formal M&S education now exist. These include programs at Old Dominion University, the Naval Postgraduate School, the University of Arizona, and the University of Central Florida.

Certification programs, of course, depend on underlying knowledge bases and primers. We recommend that

- **DMSO should convene an expert group, preferably already associated with the M&SPCC effort, to discuss the adequacy of emerging materials and requirements and the possible role of DoD in enhancing the effort.**

One way to think about this general issue is to recall personal experiences working with highly talented hackers who produced imaginative and useful code that soon fell into disrepair or otherwise proved unsustainable because talent is not enough: The building of complex models and simulations also requires discipline and solid knowledge of some basics. It is also necessary to have substantial humility and an appreciation for the kinds of subtle interactions that undercut modularity and interoperability.

A Good Overall Environment for Modeling and Simulation

Ultimately, the future of DoD-sponsored composability depends upon having a favorable environment, one that includes a strong industrial base, incentives that promote sensible developments, and mechanisms that support technically sound and fair competitions of ideas and proposals. Where it makes sense, i.e., in natural clusters of organizations working on a common problem with appropriate contractual relationships, that environment should also encourage healthy cooperation and sharing across organizations, in both government and industry.[42] Standards, addressed above, are a key element here, but many other elements apply as well. These relate to issues such as the existence of a marketplace of ideas and suppliers,

[42] This has been a major theme of past studies of data practices (Appendix C) and simulation-based acquisition (Appendix F). Many of those studies have highlighted problems of "culture."

incentives at the individual and organizational level, and a balance between maintaining long-term relationships with centers of excellence and assuring vitality with a constant inflow of ideas and challenges. Large-scale DoD M&S efforts will be enhanced by a much greater degree of commonality with the activities of the commercial sector. This will increase both options and dynamism, in part because it will be possible for good commercial-sector ideas, methods, and tools to be adapted quickly to defense applications. One possible element of "other infrastructure" would be technology and standards allowing rapid searches for potentially relevant components, and also allowing reasonably efficient zooming-in that might include running candidates against standard datasets to see whether, at least superficially, the components do what the researcher imagines they do. Being able to take next steps and to automatically evaluate possible compositions in the contexts of intended use would require more cutting-edge developments, but movement in that direction is possible.

Incentives

Conceiving standards is one thing, but success in their implementation and exploitation will depend sensitively on the incentives perceived by individuals and their organizations. The issue of model documentation provides rich examples of successes and failures. On the one hand, traditional acquisition-system requirements for by-the-book paper documentation of a sort conceived decades ago is widely recognized as having been neither wise nor effective. Costs were high, and the comprehensibility and maintainability of the product were low (without continued high costs). As users of M&S are prone to emphasize, any model or simulation that is being used will quickly depart from its documentation. This may be even more true today, as there is increased emphasis on flexibility and adaptiveness in military operations, which translates into the need for extensible M&S and, often, interactiveness.

Against this background, we note that *higher-level documentation* is often the weakest, but if it exists, it can also be the most stable. Further, when workers assemble materials for their particular system-of-systems configuration, they don't really want to be reading details of line-by-line code; they want something more abstract. They may even wish to reprogram certain modules for convenience—perhaps so as to standardize in their own environment. As a result, they particularly value higher-level documentation. This is precisely the world in which UML fits well. However, UML has a number of serious shortcomings, and developing UML representations is not always quick and easy. It is possible that by combining UML representations with more ad hoc information presented in XML or one of its variants, and by supplementing these with more rigorous treatment of the treatment of time, good, more-or-less standardized packages could prove very attractive.

A key issue at this point will be the problem of legacy code. Even if DoD could agree on sensible standards for future code, the fact is that most of the M&S that will be used years in the future will have been developed years in the past. Here we suggest that

- **DMSO should investigate the feasibility of *retrodocumenting* important models and components, using the standards (or perhaps a light version thereof) referred to above (e.g., using a synthesis of UML/XML and simulation-specific specification). Having such high- and moderate-level documentation would be quite powerful even if the only detailed "documentation" were the programs themselves.**
- **If the results of this study are encouraging, then DMSO should work with the services and other funders to assure that financial incentives are created for retrodocumenting. Funds for such work might even be made available in an OSD-controlled central pot.**

Strengthening the Industrial Base

Modeling and simulation is a huge activity; even DoD-sponsored M&S is huge (we have no figures on the costs, but they probably run into the tens of billions annually, depending on how one counts). At the same time, it appears to us that DoD's large composability-related efforts are often undertaken in a manner that places little emphasis on continuity of expertise. This is in contrast with the efforts of the Defense Advanced Research Projects Agency (DARPA), for example, which at any given time has well-recognized centers of expertise, which it funds over a significant period. It is in even greater contrast to the methods used out of self-interest in industry, where M&S capability is recognized as a critical corporate asset. We recommend that

- **DMSO should conduct an in-government study to reassess the mix of contracting vehicles that should be used, the mix of emphasis on centers of excellence and ad hoc entrepreneurial choices, etc.**
- **Depending on results, DMSO might wish to advocate an across-DoD approach that would better assure a combination of stability, innovation, and competition.**

The Bottom Line

In summary, to improve prospects for composability in its M&S, DoD should develop and communicate a set of realistic images and expectations, back away from excessive promises, and approach improvement measures as a systems problem involving actions and investments in multiple areas ranging from science and technology to education and training. Most of the investments can have high leverage if commercial developments are exploited; some will be unique to DoD's particular needs.

APPENDIX A

Definitions

Basic Definitions

Definitions are always a problem. This appendix presents the definitions used in this monograph.

General Definitions

Model. The official DMSO definition of model is "a physical, mathematical, or otherwise logical representation of a system, entity, phenomenon, or process." That is a good definition for broad, inclusive purposes, but more precision is needed here. As a result, for the domain of DoD applications (rather than, say, the world of art, movies, medicine, or political science, where other meanings apply), it is useful to refer to *conceptual models* and *specified models*, as defined below. Several authors have emphasized that rigor requires what we call a specified model.[1]

A *conceptual model* is an overview of how the system being modeled is "seen" and represented. There is no universal recipe for writing a conceptual model, but the result should convey key concepts to the reader. A conceptual model might include, e.g., lists of objects and various diagrams, such as those of data flow. Although it might describe briefly how calculations are done (e.g., "the model assumes the

[1] See Zeigler, Praehofer, and Kim, 2000, which specifies models using system-theory methods and builds in the concept of experimental frame; and Weisel, Petty, and Mielke, 2003, which for its purposes defines a model as a computable function over a set of inputs, a set of outputs, and a non-empty set of states.

Lanchester square law"), it would not ordinarily be comprehensive, nor would it spell out the details. Good conceptual models are extremely important for communication.

A *specified model* (or, in most of this monograph, simply "model") is, at a minimum, a specification of behavior (i.e., the outputs for given inputs). The specification can be more detailed, defining, e.g., the model's objects, their attributes, and the processes that determine changes of their states. In any case, the specification must be sufficient to permit implementation, typically with a computer program. Ideally, the model should be independent of any particular programming language, although it will reflect one or another formalism, such as differential equations, difference equations, or—to illustrate something quite different—decision tables describing notional human reasoning.

Some specified models may be good conceptual models, and some conceptual models may pretty well specify everything, but more typically the two types look rather different from each other.

A *dynamic model* is a model of a time-dependent system. Dynamic models are used in simulations (and may then be called simulation models), which generate modeled system behavior over time.

A *simulator* is a mechanism, typically a computer program, for implementing or executing a model. Early flight simulators, in contrast, were basically hardware. Today's simulators may involve a mixture of hardware (e.g., realistic command-and-control display screens) and software (e.g., mechanisms for "stimulating" the user with realistic tracks and the like, which are actually model-generated).

Simulation is experimentation with a dynamic model, i.e., with a simulation model. Sometimes the word *simulation* is used in other ways, as when referring to a particular computer code. Ambiguity can be avoided by using the term *simulation model* or *simulation program* instead.

An *experimental frame* defines the context in which simulation occurs. The experimental frame can be regarded as a system in itself, a system that interacts with the simulation and the referent, which may be the real-world system or another simulation regarded as correct.

Specifying an experimental frame may include indicating objectives, the acceptable domain of inputs, various assumptions and constraints (e.g., behavior of satellites in outer space rather than in the inner atmosphere), and even the way in which users will operate on output data to generate whatever they actually need for their applications. This could be as detailed as noting that the simulation's results will be used only to generate a particular PowerPoint viewgraph. The reason for all this is that the "validity" of a simulation depends on such details. Even Newton's laws are not valid everywhere (e.g., when objects' velocities approach the speed of light or when one is dealing with some atomic and molecular phenomena).[2]

Figure A.1 indicates the relationships. The real system (or some other referent, such as another model considered to be correct) is represented by a model, which is executed by a simulator (e.g., a computer program running on a particular computer, or a hardware simulator). How well the model represents the referent is one issue; how well the simulator executes the model is another; and how well the simulator generates behavior like that of the real system is yet another, although closely related to the first two. To assess the goodness of relationships, one needs to specify context and criteria. This is the function of an experimental frame.[3] Figure A.1 indicates an overall experimental frame around all three of the constructs but then shows more-focused frames around pairs. One of the general points here is that to assess the quality of any of the relationships shown, it is necessary to specify context, such as the domain of relevant inputs, the ac-

---

[2] When we first encountered the terminology of *experimental frame* some years ago, we were inclined to prefer something that sounded less technical, such as *context*. That may be acceptable for informal conversation or high-level briefings, but we have been convinced of the need to highlight the point that the experimental frame must itself be a rigorous concept to be specified. Otherwise, discussion of issues such as the validity of a composite system remains dysfunctionally imprecise. For example, senior officials being briefed on a model's applicability may be told that it has been validated for purposes of weapon-system acquisition, but that would be absurd. Rather, one should ask, "Acquisition of what system, to have what capabilities, for what range of circumstances?"

[3] The concept of experimental frame was introduced by Bernard Zeigler in the 1970s (see Zeigler, Praehofer, and Kim, 2000). This discussion is our own, however, and it differs from the usual one in some respects.

Figure A.1
Validating a Model Within an Experimental Frame

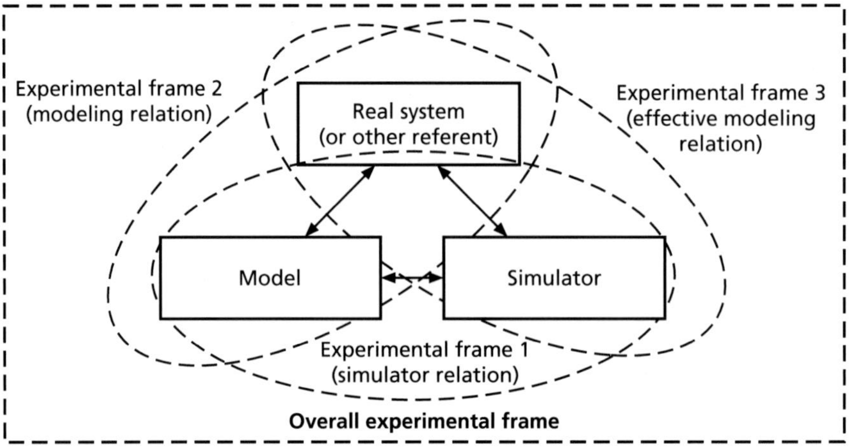

RAND *MG101-A.1*

curacy and resolution needed for the application, and so on. Specifying such matters meaningfully is the job of experimental frames.

Another general point here is that even if one believes a model represents the referent pretty well for a given purpose, the simulator (e.g., a computer program that uses numerical integration rather than continuous equations) may introduce unacceptable errors. *Verification* is about assuring that this does not happen. And even if one believes that the model is pretty good and that the simulator executes it properly, the ultimate test of a simulation is to compare its predictions with those of the referent under controlled circumstances. That is what people normally think of as "validation," although in practice validation involves a mix of many activities. After all, it is usually not possible to exercise the referent system rigorously. Instead, one may have only limited experimental data from imperfectly recorded situations. Thus, validation may include, for example, looking at the modeling relation closely (e.g., looking at the algorithms and relating them to settled theory) and having experts assess the apparent reasonableness of generated behavior for a well-chosen set of conditions. Bigelow and Davis, 2003, discusses defining "validation" for cases in which the model's data are very uncertain.

These matters have been extensively discussed in prior work for DMSO and in the literature. We believe, however, that the need to distinguish the elements of Figure A.1 from each other and to make evaluations within well-defined experimental frames has been much underappreciated. For example, meaningful validation may prove difficult or impossible because discrepancies are caused by a complex mixture of errors in the modeling relationship and the simulator relationship, because information about the referent system was obtained under conditions that bear an uncertain relationship to those used in the simulation, or because there are stochastic factors at work.

Composability-Related Definitions

A *module* is a self-contained unit that is independently testable and usable in a variety of contexts. A module interacts with its environment only through a well-defined interface of inputs and outputs. If a module is part of a larger model, the only information received from or given to other elements of the model is the module's formal inputs and outputs. Thus, the rest of the model sees the module as a black box.

Simple versions of modules are so familiar that we are barely aware of them. In a given programming language, for example, one might at any point in a program compute the area A of a triangle with base 4 and height 6 by invoking a function TRIAREA as follows:

Let Paint_needed=TRIAREA(4,6)*paint_per_square_foot.

The function TRIAREA would be defined somewhere in the overall model as

TRIAREA(Base, Altitude)

Definition: Base*Altitude/2

In this case, the module is trivial and the inputs and outputs say it all, except for the formula itself. Sometimes, however, a module can be quite complex. The Solver optimization program in Microsoft Excel is a sophisticated piece of software with proprietary algorithms inside. The user merely selects the cells that represent input parameters to the calculation that are to be varied and the cell containing the result of the calculation and invokes Solver, which varies the parameter values systematically to come up with estimates of the optimum set of values. Solver can be invoked anywhere within an Excel program.

In normal English, a *component* may simply be a "part" of a larger model, with no implications about whether the "part" is truly separable. For example, we may think of a modem as a component of our laptop, but if the modem is damaged, we may find that repairing it entails replacing the motherboard as well (much to our surprise, in a recent case).

So much for the layman's definition. In the context of this monograph, and in most discussions of composability, a component is a module that can be reused—not only within a given computer program, but also in other, similar programs, or even in very different ones. Some people have even more in mind, and when they use the term *component,* they are thinking of a reusable module for which there are alternatives, competition, and a market.

Szyperski defines a software component as follows:

> software component: a unit of composition with contractually specified interfaces and explicit context dependencies only. A software component can be deployed independently and is subject to composition by third parties (Szyperski, 2002, p. 41).

Szyperski also mentions that components are independently produced and acquired (Szyperski, p. xxii). He emphasizes that for components to be particularly valuable, i.e., to have a multiplier effect in development, there needs to be competition for both function and price (p. xxii). That is, the component should compete in a commercial marketplace. Software components, however, are not at all the same thing as model components, and it remains to be seen how well the software analogy will carry over.

Relationship of Modules and Components

Components, as that term is used in the context of composability, are modules, but most modules are not components. Modules need not be reusable by third parties, for example, and the term *module* implies nothing about independent production, acquisition, or marketing. Modularity is a broad and powerful concept in general systems work.[4] Related concepts are sometimes called *packages* (an Ada terminology), and object-oriented approaches to modeling emphasize particular kinds of modules based on classes.

Composability

With this background of basic definitions, we consider composability to be the capability to select and assemble components in various combinations to satisfy specific user requirements meaningfully. A defining characteristic of composability is the ability to combine and recombine components into different systems for different purposes.[5]

The word *meaningfully* is shorthand here for noting that it is one thing to connect components so that the composition "runs," but it is quite another for that composition to be sound, as discussed below.

Defining Syntax, Semantics, and Contextual Validity

It is usually said that composability is affected by syntactic and semantic problems. What follows is a homely example, using the familiar first-year physics problem of a falling body, which highlights a third problem. Suppose we consider combining two models, A and B, both of which purport to describe the speed of two types of falling body, because the composite model is estimating damage that a vehi-

---

[4] For extensive discussion with numerous examples, see Baldwin and Clark, 2000. One strong feature of this book is separate discussions of splitting a system into modules, substituting one modular design for another, augmenting a system by adding a module, excluding a module from a system, inverting to create new design rules, and porting a module to another system. All of these matters are quite relevant to the software aspects of composability.

[5] This definition is that of Petty and Weisel, 2003, except that we added the term *meaningfully*.

cle might suffer if it were hit by various falling bodies. Can we include both models in a larger model, or can we choose to use either A or B without problems?

Model A computes the speed V(t) for times less than T*, where T* is the time at which the body strikes the ground. The equations might be as follows:

Inputs: initial altitude Y_0, drag coefficient D, and acceleration of gravity g

$$V(t) = \int_0^t [g - DV(s)]ds \text{ for } t < T^*$$

$$V(t) = 0 \text{ for } t \geq T^*$$

$$0 = Y_0 - \int_0^{T^*} V(s)ds$$

$$Y(t) = Y_0 - \int_0^{T^*} V(s)ds \text{ for } t < T^*$$

$$Y(t) = 0 \text{ for } t \geq T^*$$

Outputs: T*, V(t), Y(t)

Now suppose that model B contains its own treatment of the falling-body problem, with the relevant equations being

Inputs: initial altitude H_0, acceleration of gravity a, drag coefficient D, and body cross-section S

$$V(t) = \int_0^t [a - DSV(s)]ds \text{ for } V(s) < \frac{a}{DS}$$

$$V(t) = V_{ss} \text{ for } t \geq T_{ss}$$

T_{ss} is defined by

$$a - DSV(t = T_{ss}) = 0$$

$$V_{ss} = V(t = T_{ss}) = \frac{a}{DS}$$

$$H(t) = H_0 - \int_0^t V(s)ds \text{ for } t < T_{impact}$$

$$H(t) = 0 \text{ for } t \geq T_{impact}$$

$$T_{impact} \approx H_0 / V_{ss}$$

Outputs: T_{ss}, V_{ss}, T_{impact}, $V(t)$, $H(t)$

In comparing the two models and thinking about whether they can be combined (model A used for some objects, model B used for others), or whether either can be substituted for the other, we should recognize three types of problem: syntax, semantics, and validity.

Syntax

First, models A and B have different names for the same concepts: acceleration of gravity, initial altitude, and impact time. However, making the names consistent is trivial.

Semantics

Both models have mostly the same semantics, in that they mean the same thing by initial altitude and the acceleration of gravity, speed versus time, and so on. Note, however, that the drag coefficients D in the two models are different, even thought they both have the same symbol D and the same name. Model B's drag coefficient has been normalized for a unit area of falling-body cross-section. Thus, model A's D is the same conceptually as model B's DS. One might conclude, therefore, that one could connect the two models meaningfully.

Validity

Assuming, however, that one has worked out differences in notation and meaning, as indicated above, there is an additional problem. Model B uses an approximation in calculating the time of impact, an approximation that assumes that the body reaches steady-speed velocity quickly enough so that the average speed from the start of the problem until impact is just that steady-speed velocity. Clearly, that might be a reasonable approximation for some types of bodies and some initial altitudes. However, it might be a very bad approximation in other cases. Suppose, for example, that model A was developed with rather spherical objects in mind and model B was developed for more pointy objects. Depending on circumstances, the latter's objects might never reach steady-state velocity, and the average speed enroute to impact might better approximate $gT^*/2$.

Semantic Confusion About the Meaning of Semantics

The principal reason for the example given above is to point out that the word *semantics* is itself ambiguous. Computer scientists not uncommonly use it to mean everything except syntax.[6] Thus, the contextual "validity" issue would be subsumed in referring to semantic issues. That usage is surely defensible,[7] but it is hardly the way many—and perhaps most—of us use the term. We prefer to use *semantics* to refer to the "meaning" of the symbols (see on-line Merriam Webster dictionary),[8] which is also consistent with the original Greek root. Thus, in the above example, both models may mean precisely the same thing by *impact time*, but model A calculates it differently than does model B, and even if both models are sufficiently valid for

---

[6] Philosophy-of-language authors refer to syntax, semantics, and *pragmatics*, where the latter refers to the context-dependence of meaning. Context could include speaker identity, time of utterance, tacit information, pitch, irony, etc. (examples suggested to us by Phillip Hammond). See also Brown, 2003, for some good examples. Here, for brevity only, we consider *pragmatics* to be subsumed under *semantics*.

[7] See Weisel, Petty, and Mielke, 2003, for a theoretical discussion of the validity of compositions in which composability is treated as having two forms, syntactic and semantic.

[8] We acknowledge, however, that the Microsoft Word dictionary includes, as a third definition, "relating to the conditions in which a system or theory can be said to be true."

the contexts in which they were first developed, one of them is likely to be wrong in some circumstances.

This strikes us as important because saying that composability requires working the problems of syntax and semantics makes it sound too easy: One can work the syntax problems and have consistency of "meaning," yet have an invalid composition. Another reason for our position is that "validity" is seldom an intrinsic characteristic of a model or simulation, but rather is a property of a comparison in a particular context. For example, if one has data for a common context on a real-world system's behavior and a simulation's behavior, then one might be able to conclude that using the simulation is sufficiently accurate for a particular application in that context. That is, the simulation is "valid" in that context. One could not have inferred this validity by merely looking at the simulation's code and understanding thoroughly all of its variables and data, or even by doing that plus having information on its validation for the situations (presumably different) that its original developers had in mind.[9]

One criticism that may be levied against our calling out validity separately is that semantics, as discussed by computer scientists, has many components. Why call out validity separately, but not the others? Appendix C discusses the many levels of semantic compatibility, but concludes—as we do—that it still falls short of fully covering validity. Others will parse the problem differently.

---

[9] This problem does not arise in Weisel, Petty, and Mielke, 2003, because the authors are essentially proving, for some cases, that simulation components valid according to a contextually meaningful metric can be composed while preserving that validity. For their purposes, they do not need to confront the problem of having components with validities established only for cases different from the ones in which the composed simulation will be used.

APPENDIX B

The Elusive Nature of Components

Jeff Rothenberg

Introduction

Component-based programming, or software engineering, has been something of a holy grail for several decades (although it has acquired its current name only recently). Most attempts at creating component marketplaces have failed, but the goal continues to be deemed worthy of pursuit, despite these failures. Among the earliest success stories about widely reusable components were the well-known scientific subroutines developed for early FORTRAN environments. These proved capable of widespread use with little or no modification; yet subsequent attempts to create components embodying analogous kinds of capabilities in a wide range of programming languages and environments have typically been unsuccessful. Either the resulting components have not turned out to be generic enough to be widely used, or they have been too complex to use effectively.

The most obvious difference between the FORTRAN scientific subroutines and the many failed attempts at producing components is that the former have uniquely well-defined functions and interfaces. For example, it is relatively simple to define the necessary arguments and intended behavior of a cosine function unambiguously, whereas the intended behavior of something like a general-purpose graphical-interface widget may be much more debatable. Simulation models tend to be very complex programs with relatively ill-defined behavior and therefore inhabit the opposite end of the spectrum from the cosine function.

The usual approach to defining a component is to consider it to be a black box whose internal workings are hidden and whose behavior is fully specified by its interface. However, this assumes that each component is a separable entity that can be used meaningfully without understanding how it works. While this may be true for the cosine function, it is rarely true of simulation models. Furthermore, the impetus for composing simulation models is not always to combine disjoint functions that are modeled in disjoint regions of simulation space: Rather, it may be to combine different phenomena or behaviors of related or distinct entities that interact in the same region of simulation space. In such cases, it is unrealistic to expect the overall behavior of the intended composed model to factor along clean lines that correspond to those of existing component models; yet if it is impossible to factor the overall simulation this way, then component models may have to interact with each other in highly nonmodular ways that defy the definition of clean interfaces. This is especially true if component models are not designed to be composed with each other but are composed after the fact, in ad hoc ways that were not anticipated when the models were designed.

Semantic Description of Models as Components

Several levels of understanding and agreement are required between two models in order for them to be meaningfully composed—that is, for their composition to produce meaningful results. For convenience, we will call these *composability levels.* First, the models must be able to connect to each other so that they can exchange bits. Next, they must agree on the data types and the packaging of the data and control information represented by the bits they exchange. Then, they must agree on the interpretation of their exchanged information, for example, that a given data item represents speed in knots or meters per second. Furthermore, they must agree on the underlying meaning of their exchanged data, for example, that the speed of movement of a battalion means the speed with which the centroid of its forces moves. This "meaning" level may need to include an understanding of the algorithms, constraints, and context used to compute the exchanged data; for example, if simulation time is exchanged between two models, it may be crucial for each model to understand whether the other considers time to be continuous or discrete and, if discrete, whether it is clock-based, event-based, etc. Finally, the models must understand each other's overall function and purpose and must determine that it makes sense for them to be composed with one another.

This need for understanding and agreement at multiple composability levels is akin to the seven-layer open systems interconnect (OSI) network model, in which connectivity occurs at a number of levels simultaneously. To some extent, all of the above levels of agreement are needed even if models are simply intended to interoperate with each other, i.e., to exchange and use each other's results. Yet composability often implies a more intimate relationship than simple interoperation: Composed models may be asked to function as a single model that combines features and capabilities of its components or exhibits new, "emergent" behavior that is more than just the sum of its parts.

These composability levels represent different aspects of run-time interoperability. Yet before two models can be connected at run time, they (or their users) must determine whether they can and should be composed. This normally requires whoever is configuring a composed M&S effort to understand the functions and purposes of each available component model and to determine which of them can and should be composed to produce the desired overall functionality and behavior. In some cases, this might be done by automated M&S agents, but these would still need to be driven by human input that specifies the purpose of the desired composition. This configuration-time process need not actually connect the models to be composed, but it must determine which component models are necessary and appropriate for the composition—and that they can be meaningfully connected. Although some of this configuration process might be performed on the fly (i.e., just before or even during run time), its first phase, at least, is more likely to be performed "off-line" by humans who evaluate available models as candidate components for a desired composition. Nevertheless, whenever it is performed, this configuration process will require information about component models at all of the composability levels discussed above.

Multilevel composability information about each component model is therefore needed for both configuration and run-time purposes. However, while off-line configuration can in principle utilize traditional forms of documentation, run-time composition and mediation require that information about each composability level be available in machine-readable form so that it can be processed by an M&S composition environment, such as HLA. Furthermore, traditional textual documentation of models has often proved lacking when it is used to try to determine whether existing models are meaningfully composable. This is due to the informality of such documentation, which makes it ambiguous and incomplete. It would therefore be desirable to represent composability information in a formal way, both to ensure that it has rigorous, unambiguous semantics and to make it machine-readable so that it can be used by automated agents, whether at configuration time or run time.

The need for formal information describing components has been recognized in many component-based efforts, including CORBA and Jini. As in the M&S composition case discussed here, this information is often thought of as enabling both discovery of appropriate components (i.e., to support configuration) and more-or-less automated connection and mediation of those components at run time. If such information were available for models, it could be used for various purposes, including

- Finding and matching candidate models for composition.
- Inferring limits of use and interpretation of federations.
- Run-time translation among disparate models.

At least four activities are required to produce and utilize formal composability information of the kind envisioned here:

1. A formalism should be defined that has sufficient expressive power to describe the necessary aspects of models and that enables the

kinds of inference needed to use such information both to determine at configuration time whether models can be composed meaningfully and appropriately for a given purpose and to create and mediate that composition at run time.
2. Using the formalism developed in (1), an ontology should be defined that formalizes the kinds of composability information discussed above.
3. Candidate component models should be described in terms of the formal ontology defined in (2).
4. Tools should be developed to perform the kinds of inferences needed to utilize the knowledge developed in (3) to aid in making intelligent configuration-time and/or run-time decisions about composing candidate models.

The development of formalisms is an ongoing area of research which appears to be bearing new fruit in the form of several efforts that utilize XML as an overall encoding language. It should be noted that XML by itself provides only a small part of activity (1) above, since XML is essentially a generic mechanism in which formalisms can be defined. Similarly, many so-called "semantic web" efforts, such as XMSF (extensible modeling and simulation framework) and modeling, virtual environments, and simulation (MOVES) at the Naval Postgraduate School address only a part of (1). Efforts like DAML-OIL and OWL, on the other hand, appear to offer good starting points for (1), although they do not address (2) through (4). Ongoing work in architecture-description languages (ADLs), such as Acme and Wright, aim at (1) and (2) for general architectural components but do not specifically address M&S issues. In the M&S realm, recent versions of the DEVS formalism provide for modularity and integration with HLA (DEVS/HLA), but DEVS does not spell out a formal language with the expressivity needed for (1), and it addresses (2) through (4) only to a very limited extent.[1] The HLA object model

[1] The system entity structure (SES) associated with the DEVS methodology does, however, provide a partial ontology that can be quite useful in organizing component models in a

template (OMT) can be thought of as an attempt to address (1) and (2), but its expressivity appears to be sharply limited with respect to the full range of purposes discussed here.

Significant effort would be required to perform (2) through (4) to the depth envisioned here. Doing so seems necessary but not sufficient to ensure the composability of models, since the many other issues raised in this monograph would still have to be addressed. In particular, the validity of a composed model cannot be guaranteed by the kinds of composability information suggested here: We are still a long way from being able to prove the validity of a model formally, let alone being able to compose such proofs to infer the validity of a composition of provably valid models.

To summarize, the meaningful composition of models requires that their behavior along a number of dimensions be understood and characterized in a formal way that avoids the ambiguity of textual documentation and enables automated processes to configure, compose, and mediate component-based simulations. As emphasized throughout this monograph, there are many aspects to understanding and characterizing models in this way, some of which involve fundamental scientific or mathematical understanding that does not yet exist. However, even if such understanding can be obtained, it must still be formalized and encoded in an appropriate ontology so as to be sharable among models that are to be composed.

---

repository and going about hierarchical composition (see Zeigler, Praehofer, and Kim, 2000).

APPENDIX C

Shared, Accessible Data for Composability

Conclusions from a Workshop

Although the "data problem" is not discussed at any length in this monograph, it clearly remains fundamental, as part of the overall effort to achieve greater reusability and composability. The problem involves "stovepiped" data files whose very existence remains unknown to those who might need them, and a lack of metadata describing the content, accuracy, timeliness, and context for data. The state of data practices and recommendations was reviewed in a Military Operations Research Society (MORS) meeting on "Improving Defense Analysis Through Better Data Practices," held March 25–27, 2003 (see Allen and Simpkins, 2003).

Table C.1, adapted from the report of the synthesis panel that was part of the workshop, shows many parallels with the issues of composability. These recommendations indicate the rather fundamental difficulties remaining before self-describing and self-documenting data can become widely available for composing models and simulations.

A recent briefing provides insight into metadata standards being developed within DoD to help alleviate the above problems.[1] The preliminary "core discovery metadata standard" described therein (chart 10) indicates that metadata should exist in five categories:

---

[1] Simon (undated briefing).

Table C.1
Recommendations of a MORS Panel on Data Practices

Culture	• A *fundamental* change in the data culture is required (e.g., power is derived from *sharing*, not *hoarding,* data)
	• Accelerate actions (e.g., meetings, coordination efforts, socialization) to *break down barriers with the diverse communities* that must participate in the data enterprise
People: Analysts	• Develop curricula, programs to *enhance education and training for the military operations analyst*, emphasizing the criticality of data in the analysis process
People: Decision-makers	• Institutionalize the commitment of senior decisionmakers to addressing the data problem
	• Provide decisionmakers with a list of data-related questions that they should pose to the analyst team
Organization	• Establish organizational mechanisms to encourage inter-agency, international cooperation on data sharing
Policies	• Reassess existing policies which severely restrict the flow of data and information across institutional barriers, rebalancing security concerns and the "need to know" (Should we reexamine the existing "need to know" policy, in which there is a presumption of guilt, rather than innocence?)
Tools	• Expand the analyst's "tool chest" to support the collection, generation, conversion, verification and validation (V&V), and visualization of data
Processes	• Develop a data-support business process that exploits strengths (e.g., encourages the generation of metadata) and ameliorates weaknesses (deals with disincentives such as proprietary concerns)
	• Convene a NATO studies, analysis, and simulation (SAS) panel to develop an alliance code of best practices (CoBP) on data for analysis (analogous to C2 assessment and operations other than war (OOTW) CoBPs)
Products	• Perform pilot studies to clarify the desired attributes of the analytic baselines
	• Continue to establish repositories and data warehouses to archive and provide access to verified and validated data for those with a validated need

- *Security layer*. Detailed security markings layer. Obligation based on top-level security classification found in the resource description layer.
- *Resource description layer*. Resource maintenance and administration metadata (e.g., data created, author, publisher, type, security classification, etc.).
- *Format description layer*. Format-specific metadata (e.g., picture size, database record count, multimedia stream duration, file size, etc.).
- *Content description layer*. Rich content descriptive metadata structure. Structured approach to provide robust method for discovery.
- *Community-of-interest-defined layers*. Metadata structure(s) defined by community of interest (COI). Must be registered with DoD XML Registry for integration with enterprisewide capabilities. Will define requirements for "enterprise-certified" COI layers (e.g., need some rules to ensure proper usage).
-

That same briefing indicates that the DoD Metadata Registry is based on the ISO 11179 specification for metadata registries and incorporates linkages to a variety of existing metadata resources such as the DoD XML Registry, the Defense Data Dictionary System (DDDS), and commonly used data reference sets.

We conclude that a basis is being laid within DoD for metadata of critical importance for composable models and simulations but that substantial problems remain before the availability and effective use of metadata will be possible. One website with many relevant links is http://www.diffuse.org/alpha.html.

A Process-Engineering View of the Challenge

One interesting feature of the data-practices workshop was discussion by the synthesis working group of a holistic way of viewing how to go about improving prospects for data practices. That view was derived from ideas of business process reengineering. A slightly modified version of the depiction used in the workshop is given in Figure C.1, which describes the setting and was suggested by Stuart Starr as a variant that might apply to composability. It can be seen as a business process reengineering view. It conveys the sense that to make changes, one must address *all* of the components. After all, composability activities occur within a larger culture, one made up of people who exist in organizations. A given organization can change its processes, reallocate resources, and work on aspects of relevant science, technology, and systems. However, the effects must occur through changes in the behavior of people and the nature of the background culture. The concepts here are all multifaceted. For example, the figure shows a single culture, but a number of relevant cultures exist. DoD's industrial base consists of companies that are strongly motivated by concerns about profitability, which in turn lead to proprietary practices. Within the companies are researchers who are not only part of their corporate culture, but also professionals (e.g., analysts or modelers) with associated codes of ethics and motivations. Many of the relevant figures are military officers, who certainly exist in a distinct culture.

Figure C.1
A Holistic Process-Engineering View

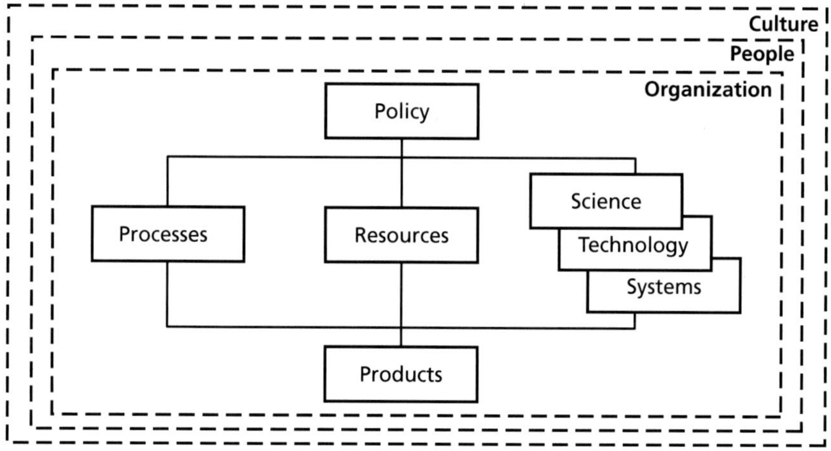

RAND *MG101-C.1*

They also, however, have professional motivations. And so on. If we equate "organization" in the figure with DoD, then DoD can effect change by promulgating appropriate policies and processes, allocating resources, and investing in science, technology, and systems. Some of this will lead to products, such as tools and infrastructure.

This view of the problem has a significant overlap with that used in the present monograph. Indeed, our conclusions and recommendations address all of the elements of Figure C.1.

APPENDIX D

Subtleties of Composition Related to Model Specification for Simulation

Purpose

The purpose of this appendix is to illustrate simply that (1) a black-box depiction of a would-be component may be quite deceptive when the component is being considered for use in a larger model; (2) careful composition may require addressing some internals of the black box rather than accepting a "wrapped" component on faith; and (3) specifying a *dynamic* model is trickier than one might expect from higher-level graphical depictions, especially if it is important to assure that a simulator will correctly reproduce the intended order of events. To illustrate these points we construct and solve a toy problem.

The Problem

Let us suppose that we wish to compose a model of a duel between two shooters, A and B. An umpire is tasked with dropping a flag, at which time the duelists are free to engage. One complication is that a crow is flying around and may obstruct the vision of one or both shooters, temporarily delaying knowledge that the flag has been dropped. Analytically, the problem is at least superficially similar to a rapid engagement of two opposing weapon systems (e.g., a friendly and an enemy tank that come simultaneously into an area where they are free to shoot at each other, but one is slower in seeing the other, being ordered to fire, or deciding to fire). For the purpose of illustration, however, let us focus on the toy problem.

Looking for Possible Components

Finding a Candidate

Imagine that a web search reveals a candidate component to exploit. Figure D.1 describes the inputs and outputs in a black-box depiction of that component, which we call M. The associated description might be as follows:

The Rapid-Shot Model

ZYX Corporation

> *The ZYX Corporation is a a consulting company specializing in work for police forces. The component model that we describe here and offer for reuse by others stemmed from a ZYX study that we did for a metropolitan police force on the value of quick decisionmaking and high-velocity rounds in a police situation in which an officer breaks into a room quickly to apprehend a criminal.*
>
> *For the original study, it was assumed that the officer achieves some level of surprise, but the criminal may try to shoot the officer, in which case the officer must kill the criminal before the criminal fires. If the criminal merely throws up his hands, there is no issue, but if he intends to engage, the officer will have very little time. We assumed that the officer might have only about a second in which to act. This allowed us to estimate needs for reaction time and munition speed.*
>
> *The component being offered for use is a "wrapped" version of the original. It omits some proprietary details but is thought to be useful by itself. This model computes the time, if any, at which a shooter kills a target. Inputs describe the time of the decision to shoot, the time, if any, at which the shooter is hit (relative to the order), the distance to the target, and the speed of the munition over the range to the target. The wrapped model is a simple black box with the inputs and outputs indicated. The model has been verified and validated.*

Figure D.1
Black-Box Depiction of Model M

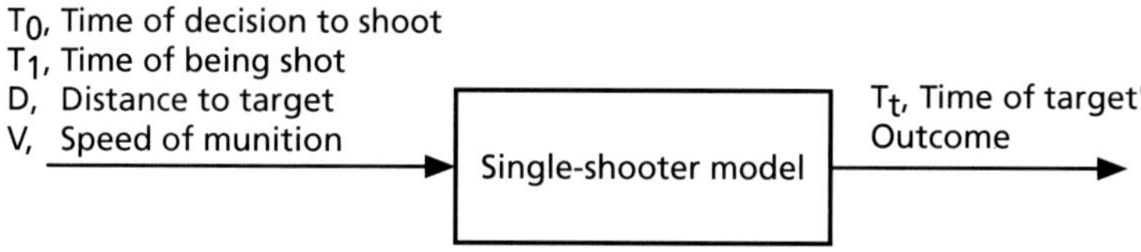

RAND *MG101-D.1*

Reading all this, it seems that the component might work for us. We download it to investigate further.

Testing the Component

Before proceeding with composition, we do some simulation experiments to see how the black-box model works and to determine whether it gives reasonable answers. One set of results is shown in Table D.1 (results for a bullet speed of 500 ft/sec).[1] We see that with 1 second in which to act before being hit (right column), the shooter can both kill the target and live. That seems consistent with the model documentation. On the basis of this and some other experiments, the results seem reasonable, so we continue.

Table D.1
An Outcome Based on a Wrapped Version of Model M

	Time Shooter is Hit (time of being shot) (sec)		
Distance (ft)	**0.5**	**0.75**	**1**
15	Shooter fails and dies	Shooter kills target and lives	Shooter kills target and lives
25	Shooter fails and dies	Shooter kills target and lives	Shooter kills target and lives
50	Shooter fails and dies	Shooter kills target but dies	Shooter kills target and lives

NOTE: Assumes a munition speed of 500 ft/sec and an order to shoot at time 0.

[1] To develop this appendix, we built and exercised the model in Analytica, which provides graphical modeling, array mathematics, built-in statistical functions, and a simplicity comparable to that of spreadsheets.

Creating a Composed Model with Two Shooters

A Naïve First Cut with Semantic Problems

It would seem that this same component model M could be used for both shooters, A and B, although adjustments would be needed to differentiate between them and to relate the original model to the concept of a duel with a troublesome crow. More specifically, we can compose a model consisting of two versions of model M. Since M's inputs are an ordered set,

[Time of decision to shoot, Time of being shot, Distance to target, Speed of munition],

we can use M for Shooter A by filling M's input slots as follows:

$$[T_{0+}T_{da}, T_0+T_{db}+D/V_a, D, V_a],$$

where

T_0 is the time that the flag is dropped, and $T_{0+}T_{da}$ is the time at which A knows to shoot, having suffered a delay T_{da} due to the crow; this sum seems to be the real meaning of M's first input parameter.

$T_0+T_{db}+D/V_a$ would seem to be the time that A himself would be shot, with D being the distance between duelists and V_b being the relevant munition speed.

D would apply for the third slot as well.

V_a would be the munition speed for Shooter A.

The outputs of M for Shooter A are [T_{B_dies}, Outcome [for A]], that is, the times at which the two shooters die.

The component model for B would be almost the same, but with inputs to M of [T_0+T_{db}, $T_0+T_{da}+D/V_b$, D] and outputs of [T_{B_dies}, Outcome [for B].]

Upon trying to make the composition work, we discover that some special tailoring is necessary, because the output "Outcome" isn't in the right form. We need to amend that function to report "A wins," "A and B die," "B wins," and "A and B survive." Thus, the outcome function is new.

Figure D.2 shows a schematic of the result. The top part of the figure shows the simple black-box depiction; the lower part of the figure gives more details. Note that because of the need for tailoring, even in this simple case, composing wasn't simply a matter of snapping things in as in plug-and-play. Only the shaded boxes indicate model reuse. Nonetheless, the composition is not very difficult. So we go ahead and implement the model.

Validity of the Naïve Composite

It may seem that the composition should obviously be valid, but let us test it. If we do so with a range of parameter values, the results may look reasonable at first, but they have some peculiarities. As shown in

Figure D.2
A Composite Model with Reuse of Model M as a Component

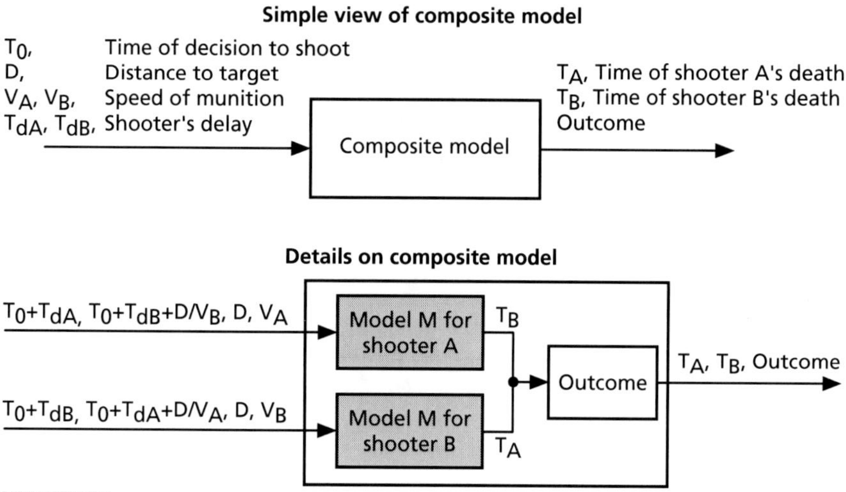

RAND *MG101-D.2*

the second column of Table D.2, if the delay encountered by Shooter A is small enough, then shooters A and B are both killed. That is, A's delay has no effect. How can that be? Also, we find that the times of death don't agree with a simple hand calculation. For a 50-ft range, a 500-ft/sec bullet would hit the target in 0.1 sec. Thus, why would there be a break point at 0.7 sec (see bottom of second column)? Perhaps a delay less than 0.1 sec would be like zero, but why 0.7 sec? Something is amiss.

"Correcting" the Naïve Composite Model

If we are semi-clever, we might infer that the black-box model has an internal representation of the time to shoot. We might then try correcting the model by adding 0.6 sec to the slots for the time a shooter is hit and the time the target is killed. This would correct the discrepancy noted above. The results improve in that they generate more-plausible kill times and more-plausible outcomes (see Table D.3). The break point occurs at a delay time of 0.1 sec, corresponding to the time for the bullet to travel to the target.

We might rationalize such a correction, while lamenting the need to make it, since there are no other blatant errors. However, we should be worried about other things that we don't understand. Was the correction truly correct, or was it just a patch of one problem, with others lurking in the background? We should also be especially worried about making relative assessments of Shooters A and B when

Table D.2
Some Results from the Naïve Composite Model

	B's Delay Time (sec)			
A's Delay Time (sec)	**0**	**0.2**	**0.7**	**0.71**
0	A and B die	A and B die	A and B die	A wins
0.2	A and B die	A and B die	A and B die	A and B die
0.7	A and B die	A and B die	A and B die	A and B die
0.71	B wins	A and B die	A and B die	A and B die

NOTE: Assumes a 50-ft distance and a bullet speed of 500 ft/sec.

Table D.3
A Corrected Naïve Composite Model

	B's Delay Time (sec)			
A's Delay Time (sec)	**0**	**0.1**	**0.3**	**0.6**
0	A and B die	A and B die	A wins	A wins
0.1	A and B die	A and B die	A wins	A wins
0.101	B wins	A and B die	A wins	A wins
0.2	B wins	A and B die	A wins	A wins
0.71	B wins	B wins	A and B die	A and B die

NOTE: Assumes a 50-ft distance and a bullet speed of 500 ft/sec.

they are described so simply (merely by differences in the delay time they suffer and the speed of their bullets). Perhaps there are other subtle differences between the shooters that should be accounted for, in which case the composite model would not be treating them fairly. What is going on *inside* the black box that we used?

Comparing Approximate and Exact Composite Models

There is reason to be concerned. Let us now suppose that we prevail upon the original builders of M to allow us to see and use the full proprietary model and to use it for composition. We can then compare results for a properly composed model to that using the wrapped component. To do this, we must specify all of the inputs to the full original component model, not just the wrapped version M used above. Table D.4 illustrates results obtained by using the default values of those hidden parameters—precisely the same values as assumed in the wrapped model. Thus, the table represents a favorable case for the comparison. Even here, there are important errors. If A is delayed by 0.2 or 0.3 sec, then the approximate composite model is wrong. Although not shown here, discrepancies worsen for other cases (e.g., with A and B having different shooting times or times to die). It seems rather evident that our naïve composite model has problems.

Table D.4
Implications of Having Used the Wrapped Model: Comparison of Results

A's Delay Time (sec)	Approximate Composite Model	Exact Composite Model
0	A and B die	A and B die
0.1	A and B die	A and B die
0.2	B wins	A and B die
0.3	B wins	A and B die
0.6	B wins	B wins
0.7	B wins	B wins

NOTE: Assumes values of 0.3 sec for each shooter's shooting time and each shooter's dying time (time to die after being hit).

With full knowledge of the underlying model, we find that the reason for the discrepancies is that the patch was a misguided guess about model internals. Implicitly, the patch assumed that the only error in the original model was in omitting the time required to shoot after a decision to do so. It also assumed that both shooters required the same time. In fact, the full model also allowed for the time after being hit for a given shooter to die. As a result, there are special cases in which the patch works, but other cases in which it does not.

Figure D.3 shows the data-flow diagram for the correct composite model. Without going through details, let us simply note that the full model must distinguish clearly between the processes of shooting and the process of dying. We shall discuss other aspects of the model later.

Implications

The point of the exercise above is that using a composite model dependent on wrapped versions of components models that we do not fully understand is neither straightforward nor good for one's nerves. Our first naïve attempt led to a manifestly invalid composite model—even though the component used was valid as initially used and seemed reasonable to use in our context. After a somewhat ad hoc correction, we had something that behaved better, but we could

Figure D.3
Data-Flow Diagram for Full Composite Model

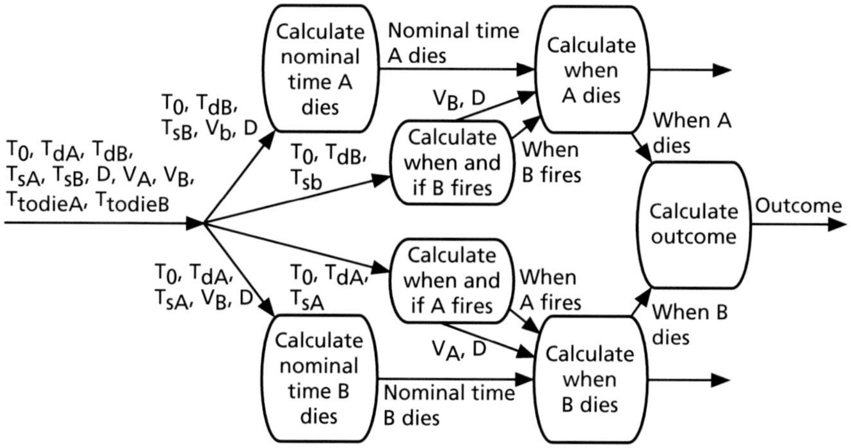

RAND *MG101-D.3*

hardly be confident about its validity. And indeed, in a test of its validity, we found discrepancies. These were hardly minor, because they dealt with who won, who survived, and who died.

None of the problems we have described are "software" problems. Nor are they simple semantic problems. All involve subtle issues of semantics and context-dependent validity.[2]

Relationship to Real-World Composability Problems

Our toy problem illustrates issues that arise more generally. DoD researchers often look at components that are large combat models in themselves but that have been wrapped so as to have a simple interface to other models. That amounts to holding a large number of input parameters constant (inside the wrapper) and using the wrapped model as a black box, much as described above. The consequences of doing so are not always straightforward to anticipate. As one example,

---

[2] The problem that was "fixed" by adding a correction term could be seen as a semantic problem in that the original component's first input actually is the time when the shooter begins shooting, not when the shot occurs. Also, the output of when the target is killed really does mean *killed*, not just hit. In the initial cut at the composite modeling (before the correction term), we were implicitly assuming that *starting to shoot* means *shoot* and *hits* means *dies*.

suppose that a good ground-forces model is to be combined with a good air-forces model. One might discover that this produces spurious results. The simple composition might have the air forces and ground forces operating much as they would have anyway, except that the ground forces cause some attrition to the air forces, and vice versa. In the real world, however, the dynamics and spatial focus of both sortie generation and maneuver would be strongly correlated. If one tried to duplicate that in the simple composite simulation, one might discover that the internals of the black-box air-forces and ground-forces models did not allow for such interactions. Perhaps the sortie-generation process amounts to nothing more than an assertion that each aircraft flies two sorties per day and that the daily sorties are spread homogeneously across the day's hours of combat. There might be no mechanisms for something more sophisticated. And perhaps the command-and-control element of the ground-forces maneuver model merely sends forces to one or another location, depending on objectives and force ratios, without regard, for example, to whether air forces might be expected to destroy bridges or cause havoc on some routes but not others.

These are the kinds of issues that analysts and modelers have to discover, negotiate, and deal with when they try to create federations of models. As with our toy problem, what seemed reasonable to hide inside a wrapper may need to be surfaced, and a good deal of tailoring may be necessary. *By and large, modelers concerned with analysis are very reluctant to use components based on wrapped models they do not fully understand. They strongly prefer having actual source code—at least to understand the components, and often because modifications are necessary.*[3]

The problem here is not complexity per se, because a modeling group building an air-ground model of combat from the outset could readily anticipate such issues and design appropriate modules from

---

[3] Some authors refer to black boxes, transparent boxes, and white boxes, where the internals of a black box are invisible, those of a transparent box are visible but not subject to change, and those of a white box can be both viewed and manipulated (see Szyperski, 2002, pp. 40–42).

the outset. The modules could then be built independently and snapped together at integration time, perhaps with relatively few corrections. Moreover, if two teams had both developed air-ground models, they might well be able to compare notes, observe that each team had some modules superior to the other's, and do some swapping—in which case one might think of the modules as components. Here the modules/components might not substitute trivially—i.e., significant reprogramming might be needed, but this type of component reuse might go reasonably well. It would not be surprising, however, if a team concluded that it would be better off taking some *ideas* and *algorithms* from the other team and then reimplementing them in the same language and style as the rest of its model. That might seem outrageous to a "software person" interested in reuse, but modelers are often much more concerned about borrowing good ideas and algorithms than about borrowing code per se. This may make sense economically as well. The time required for thinking and reworking might dominate the problem and might be increased by the complications and annoyances of dealing with foreign code, rather than just the ideas and algorithms. Further, comprehensibility, documentation, and maintenance might be simplified by the use of only one language and style.

Documentation Methods

Much has been written about documentation and the related subject of model specification and model descriptions in metadata. Our toy problem may help illustrate some of the issues. Note that the original wrapped model came with documentation that included a conceptual description and a data-flow diagram. It seemed straightforward to understand. The problem was not so much the shortcomings of the documentation as the importance of what was hidden. The documentation writers might have tried to anticipate misuse by speculating that someone might try to use the model as a component, and they would therefore have pointed out subtleties, but that is asking a lot, both socially and intellectually. The developer, for example, may have had notions about reuse in further examples involving a single shooter in more complex environments, but with the environment's parameters always being exogenous to the problem.

Another issue that arises concerns the amount and kind of documentation that can adequately specify a model for simulation in something like a federation governed by the high-level architecture. These are simulations in an object-oriented framework in which events are triggered by messages. We can use our toy problem to discuss that. In doing so, we can also discuss higher levels of detail in system specification, which is important for directing implementation and for subsequent comprehensibility.

Specifying States and Transitions

Earlier, we discussed the component model and composite model primarily in terms of inputs, outputs, and data flow. The resulting diagram (Figure D.3) is useful, but it says nothing about the algorithms internal to the processes represented by nodes, or about how a simulation (an execution of the model) might proceed. Also, the degree to which one "understands" the problem is arguably limited by the failure to look at certain details. It is often desirable to describe a model at a level of detail that includes states and state transitions. Let us elaborate with an object-oriented depiction.

Class: Referee

Object: referee [trivial in this problem]
Process: give order to shoot; maintain information on the status of the shooters over time
Message sent: shoot (with parameter representing delay in message reaching shooter, relative to T_0)

Class: Shooters

Objects: Shooter A, Shooter B
Name
Health status: alive, dying, dead
Shooting status: passive, shooting, has-shot

Process: watching for order (a null process), shooting, and dying
Messages sent: order to shoot; fact of having just fired, along with a time of impact at the target
Message received: fact of having just been hit

A variety of diagrammatic methods can be used to represent this object-oriented model. Figure D.4 shows a UML[4] state-transition diagram for either of the shooter components, expressed in object-

Figure D.4
A State Transition Diagram for Shooter A or Shooter B

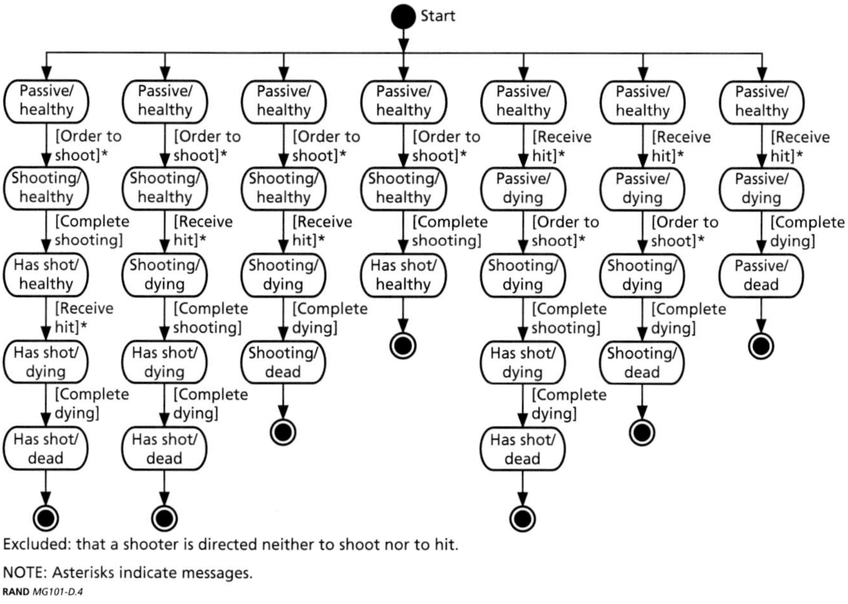

Excluded: that a shooter is directed neither to shoot nor to hit.

NOTE: Asterisks indicate messages.

RAND *MG101-D.4*

---

[4] Unified modeling language. UML is a trademark of the Object Management Group. For a brief description of UML methods, see Pfleeger, 2002, Chap. 6. Much information about UML is also available on-line (e.g., http://www.rational.com/uml/index.jsp).

oriented terms. The rounded rectangles represent composite states with abbreviated names. For example, shooting/healthy means that shooting status is *shooting* and that health status is *healthy*. The items in brackets are the events triggering the change of state. Those with asterisks are messages received, and those without correspond to the end of internal processes. Not shown are the messages sent by the shooter at each transition of state.

Such a state-transition diagram selectively provides more detail than depictions of object structure and the straightforward state transitions of a "typical" case. It is perhaps clear, however, that the detail is necessary to specify the model well enough to implement it in a simulation. Even in this toy problem, the simulation must be able to deal with no fewer than seven different transition paths for each shooter. Which path would apply depends upon the relative sizes of the various model parameters, such as time to shoot, delay time, time to die, and munition speed. Even this state-transition depiction doesn't actually specify the cases algorithmically. Someone building a simulation to execute the model, as we did, would need to do so. Moreover, in a distributed simulation environment, the simulation builder would also need to worry about issues such as latency and adjudication when two events occur at the same time. Something more detailed than this UML diagram is necessary, even in relatively high-level documentation. Moreover, the usefulness of the diagram itself is already breaking down for our toy problem, with so many paths possible. With more objects and parameters to worry about, a graphical depiction would probably not work well at all.

To illustrate the issues, let us consider briefly executing the toy problem with a discrete-time (constant time step) or a discrete-event simulation.

Discrete-Time Simulation. In a discrete-time simulation, too large a time step can sometimes lead to erroneous results. As can be seen from Figure D.4, a shooter doesn't begin dying until the clock time at which the simulation receives a message. He does not complete dying until a time step later than when he began. Thus, if the time-stepped simulation updates that object a bit later than the underlying mathematics would have had him receiving a hit, he will live longer as a result—perhaps just enough longer so that, at the next time step, he will be dying but will also complete the process of shooting. Had the time step been shorter, he might have begun dying and completed dying at time steps prior to the one at which he could complete shooting. Thus, with inappropriately large time steps, one would see errors in the fraction of cases in which one or the other shooter would live while killing the other one. The solution would be simply to use shorter time steps until answers stabilize. Table D.5 illustrates this effect. A time step of 0.05, 0.15, or even 0.5 sec is adequate, but a time step of 1 sec produces some errors (see the row for a delay time of 0.5 sec). Unfortunately, how small the time step needs to be depends on the various parameters of the problem.

Figure D.5 presents the results of Table D.5 graphically. The Y axis is a measure of the shooter's health; the x axis is time. The dark curve is for Shooter A, who is always killed if B suffers no delay. The dashed and dotted curves correspond to Shooter B in the cases where A is delayed by 0.4 and 0.5 sec, respectively. In the first case, A is just barely able to fire before dying; in the second case, A dies before he otherwise would be able to shoot. Most of the critical events are also marked on the horizontal lines marked A and B below the main graph.

At the very bottom of the figure is a time line for *apparent* events in the case in which the simulation has a time step of 1 sec. In this

Table D.5
Errors Due to Size of the Time Step in a Discrete-Time Simulation

A's Delay Time (sec)	Outcome with Time Step of 0.05 sec	Outcome with Time Step of 0.15 sec	Outcome with Time Step of 0.5 sec	Outcome with Time Step of 1 sec
0.2	Both die	Both die	Both die	Both die
0.4	Both die	Both y	Both die	Both die
0.5	**B wins**	**B wins**	**B wins**	**Both die**
0.6	B wins	B wins	B wins	B wins

NOTE: Assumes both A and B take 0.3 sec to shoot and 0.3 sec to die once hit. They are 50 ft apart and fire munitions that travel at 500 ft/sec.

Figure D.5
Event Sequences in an Illustrative Simulation

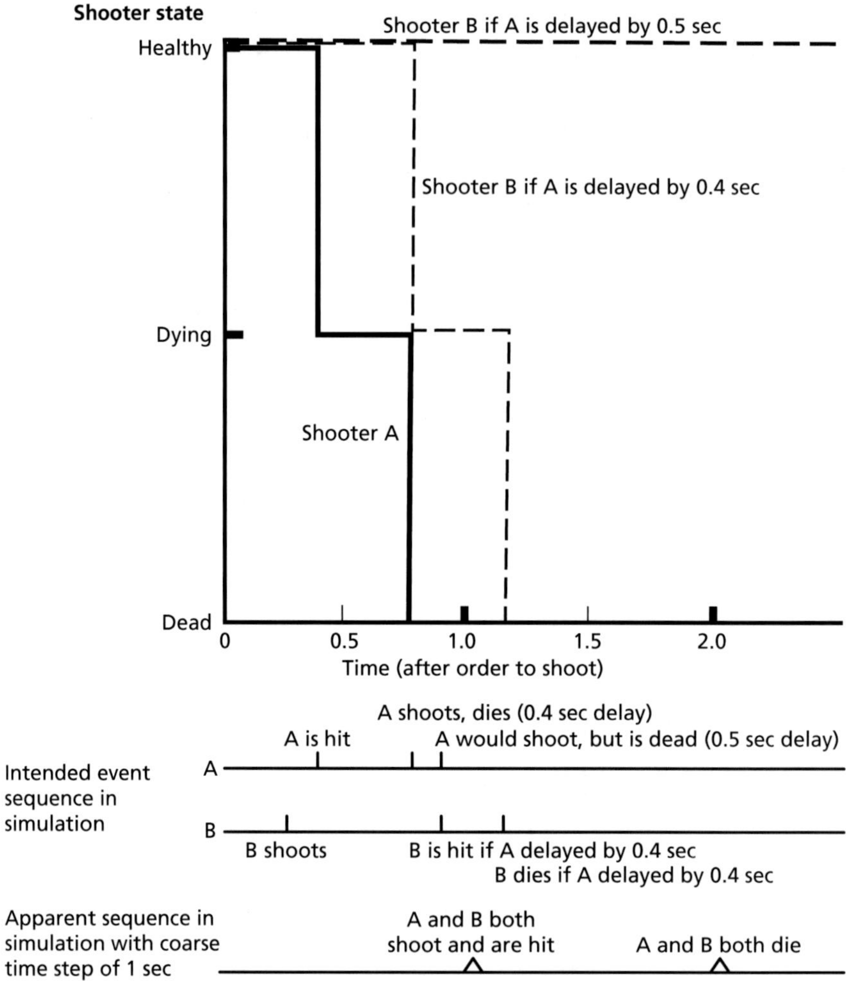

NOTE: It is assumed that both shooters take 0.3 sec to shoot and 0.3 sec to die after being shot; a shot takes 0.1 sec to reach its target; A is delayed in shooting by either 0.4 or 0.5 sec; B suffers no such delay.

RAND *MG101-D.5*

case, even though A's delay is set at 0.5 sec, at the first tick of the clock (1 sec), both shooters change state to have-shot/dying. Then, at the next tick of the clock, both die. This is an error, since, as we know from above, a more fine-grained accounting would have Shooter A die before being able to shoot. However, deep in the bowels of the simulation logic, it was assumed that a shooter cannot die until the next time step after he enters the dying state. That implementation would ordinarily be valid, but not with large time steps.[5] If we want to specify the model in a way that is simulator-independent (a good practice), then we need to flag the event details and write down the corresponding logic. Again, that is not very easy to do graphically in complex problems.

Discrete-Event Simulation. With discrete-event simulation, the logically easy solution of choosing smaller time steps until results stabilize is not available. Discrete-event simulation has many advantages, including efficiency and, some would say, a more natural correspondence to the real world in that behaviors are triggered by events rather than time per se. The simulator, however, must have an event queue and program logic to specify which event comes next in that queue. If the sequence of events depends on the relative size of multiple parameters, developing that logic will be complex and will drive a careful developer down to the kind of level suggested in Figure D.4 and beyond. In non-toy problems, the multiple possibilities would make the diagrammatic approach inappropriate, and one would be better off with a more systematic and mathematical "systems approach," such as that discussed in various places in the literature (see, e.g., Zeigler, Praehhofer, and Kim, 2000). Trying to take shortcuts or looking for a fully adequate, high-level diagrammatic specification is unlikely to be successful unless the value of the simulation does not really depend on such details of outcome. This might be the case in

---

[5] For this simple problem, if we had known that we wanted to do a simulation with a large time step, we could have included more complex logic that would have sorted out the sequence of events that occurred between time steps. More generally, that is not always possible.

some training applications, for example, but not in analysis settings.[6] For those applications, careful time management is often essential.

Conclusions

Our conclusions, then, are the following:

- The method of wrapping software components is quite powerful but is fraught with difficulties when the components are "just software." Those who use simulation for analysis should be quite cautious about composing substantive black-box models, even if the candidate components appear superficially to be suitable. DoD, on its part, should encourage greater openness about source code.
- Often, valid and understandable composition requires knowledge of the components' internals and perhaps the ability to make changes in source code.
- A key factor in improving composability is improving the quality and efficiency of documentation, particularly at a high "specification level," rather than at the level of code details.
- The methods used should include a combination of high-level graphical approaches and the more-precise, systems-oriented, atomic approaches that are needed for detailed specification relevant to time management in simulation.[7]
- The DoD simulation community, particularly those interested in distributed simulation and composability, need to agree on

[6] The investment in careful specification also pays off handsomely in composability activities, such as those practiced in Lockheed-Martin's Space Division for some years (see Appendix E). We thank Steve Hall for his demonstration and discussion of Lockheed's experience in Sunnyvale, CA, on August 5, 2003. (See also Zeigler, Hall, and Sarjoughian, 1999; and Hall, 2000.)

[7] As an example, the graphical depictions might be based on the evolving UML, whereas the more atomic and systems-oriented depictions might be based on DEVS formalism. Other candidates exist, and all of the methods have their strengths and weaknesses, as well as their advocates and detractors.

documentation methods—albeit knowing that adjustments will have to be made over time as methods evolve.

The last item is the most difficult to explain without examples, so we have presented a toy problem that illustrates how time management—a core feature of simulation—requires in practice a methodical approach to specification that identifies the many possible run-time cases and the implications of various model parameters.

APPENDIX E

Experience with Composition for Analysis

Many organizations have experience with model composability. However, to provide some concrete examples in this monograph, we have drawn on material that was readily available from a previous RAND study[1] and the work of Steven Hall at Lockheed-Martin.[2] The examples may also be of interest because the compositions were done for fundamentally *analytic* purposes, rather than as rough experimentation or training exercises.

RAND Experience with Composition of Models for Analysis

Background

RAND's suite of high-resolution models, depicted in Figure E.1, provides a unique capability for high-fidelity analysis of force-on-force encounters. In this suite, the RAND version of JANUS serves as the primary force-on-force combat-effectiveness simulation and provides the overall battlefield context, modeling as many as 1,500 individual systems on a side. The seamless model interface (SEMINT) integrates JANUS with a host of other programs into one coordinated

[1] See Davis, Bigelow, and McEver, 2001, Appendix. A much fuller description can be found in Matsumura, Steeb, Gordon, Herbert, Glenn, and Steinberg, 2001, which reviews a decade of work.

[2] See Zeigler, Hall, and Sarjoughian, 1999.

Figure E.1
RAND's Suite of High-Resolution Models

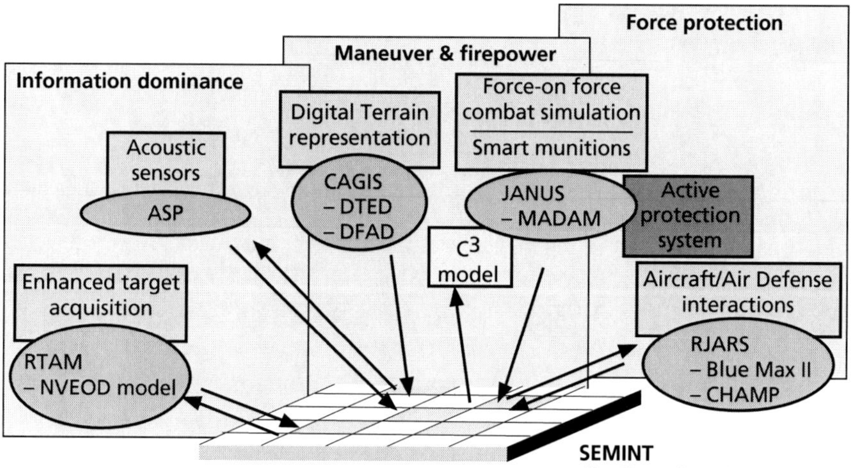

RAND *MG101-E.1*

system, even though the participating models may be written in different programming languages and may be running on different hardware under different operating systems. In effect, SEMINT provides the ability to augment a JANUS simulation by specialized high-fidelity computations of the other partaking models, without actual modification of the JANUS algorithms.

As currently configured, JANUS conducts the ground battle, calling on the RAND target acquisition model (RTAM) to provide more accurate calculation of detection probabilities of special low observable vehicles. The model to assess damage to armor by munitions (MADAM) simulates the effects of smart munitions, including such aspects as chaining logic, multiple hits, and unreliable submunitions, while the acoustic sensor program (ASP) provides a detailed simulation of acoustic phenomenology for such systems as air-delivered acoustic sensors and wide-area munitions. Should the conflict involve helicopter or fixed-wing operations, the flight planners BLUE MAX II (fixed-wing) and CHAMP (helicopter) determine flight paths for the missions, flown against the actual JANUS threat, and RAND's jamming and radar simulation (RJARS) conducts the defense against the aircraft, including detection, tracking, jamming, and surface-to-air missile (SAM) operations. The cartographic analysis and geographic information system (CAGIS) provides consistent geographic information to all the simulations, while SEMINT passes messages among the models and maintains a global virtual time to keep the models in synchronization.

Scenarios

RAND uses standard high-resolution scenarios, made available by U.S. TRADOC Analysis Center (TRAC), and modifies them as necessary to meet individual project needs. When suitable standard scenarios are not available or necessary modifications to existing scenarios are too extensive to be practical, scenarios or vignettes are developed at RAND to isolate and examine essential elements of analysis (EEA) identified for individual projects. An appropriate level of awareness of the validity of each scenario with respect to likely real-world situations and contingencies is maintained, and assumptions are always based on best available data. Vignettes are thoroughly gamed and then meticulously scripted to ensure "reasonable" tactics and behavior in the absence of human reaction and intervention, when the model suite is running in batch mode.

Although JANUS affords the capability of modeling division-versus-division-level engagements, typical vignettes are developed at the battalion task-force-versus-brigade or brigade-versus-division level. Vignettes are normally scripted to simulate 60 minutes or less of real time. In batch mode, the model suite typically runs at or faster than real time, depending upon the complexity of the vignette. (It can also be run interactively, with Red and Blue gamers.) Each vignette is iterated (nominally) 30 times to obtain a reasonable sample, and the resulting statistics are analyzed, both aggregately and by iteration.

Postprocessor

To analyze the output of the high-resolution suite, RAND has developed a postprocessor to take advantage of its enormous sorting, ordering, manipulative, and computational power for dealing with prohibitively large, free-form data sets. The software also offers a push-button-type interface for standard options programmed in SAS. This offers as close to an ideal solution as can reasonably be expected for the large datasets for each excursion in the very large analytic matrices associated with JANUS and its related models.

The postprocessor displays data in a variety of forms, from simple tables to line graphs; to pie charts; to bar and stacked bar charts; to complex, three-dimensional plots necessary for spotting trends in extremely large output datasets. It also prepares data for plotting on terrain maps in order to spot spatiotemporal relationships. These graphic displays use varying icons and colors to represent large numbers of different parameters in a single display. For example, one color may represent a battlefield system that was detected but not engaged, another may represent a system that was engaged but not killed, another may represent a system that was killed by indirect fire, and yet others may represent systems that were killed by various direct-fire weapon systems.

The postprocessor has continued to evolve as new insights from a wide-ranging variety of studies have generated new and innovative ways of viewing and presenting data from high-resolution simulations. Each time a new technique for viewing data is developed, it becomes an integral part of the postprocessor as a new push-button option.

PEM and the High-Resolution Models

Because high-resolution simulation with the JANUS suite produced some puzzling results in the study of long-range precision fires, RAND developed a low-resolution model called PEM (precision engagement model), which postulated relatively simple physics for the key engagements. PEM was then compared to and calibrated against the high-resolution models.

Only a subset of the high-resolution models are directly involved in simulating the phenomena represented in PEM, namely the effect of long-range precision fires against a specified group of target vehicles. JANUS simulates the movement of the Red vehicles. From the JANUS output, therefore, PEM obtains the Red march doctrine parameters, including the number of vehicles per packet, the separation of vehicles in a packet, the separation of packets, and the velocity of the Red vehicles. CAGIS models the terrain, providing PEM with information on the lengths of open areas. MADAM calculates the effects of long-range fires against groups of Red vehicles. SEMINT coordinates the other models.

Other high-resolution models are indirectly involved in the simulation of long-range precision fires. The Defense Science Board (DSB) '98 cases from which we took our data involved a man in the loop who decided the aimpoints and impact times of the long-range fires. He based his decisions on the simulated results of surveillance from long range by unmanned aircraft, and in different cases he received information of varying completeness. But PEM does not address the problem of deciding when or at what to shoot; as important as this aspect is in determining the overall effectiveness of long-range precision fires, it is not directly relevant to PEM.

MADAM

For PEM, the key high-resolution model is the model to assess damage to armor by munitions (MADAM). Figure E.2 illustrates its operation.

MADAM was originally written by the Institute for Defense Analyses (IDA). RAND has provided significant additional capability in the form of upgrades capable of modeling the technologies associated with the following munitions:

- Seek and destroy armor (SADARM)
- Sensor-fused weapons (SFW-Skeet)
- Damocles
- Low-cost anti-armor submunition (LOCAAS)
- Terminally guided weapon/projectile (TGW/TGP)
- Precision-guided mortar munition (PGMM) (infrared (IR) and millimeter wave (MMW))
- Brilliant anti-tank (BAT)
- Wide-area munition (WAM)

Figure E.2
Operation of MADAM

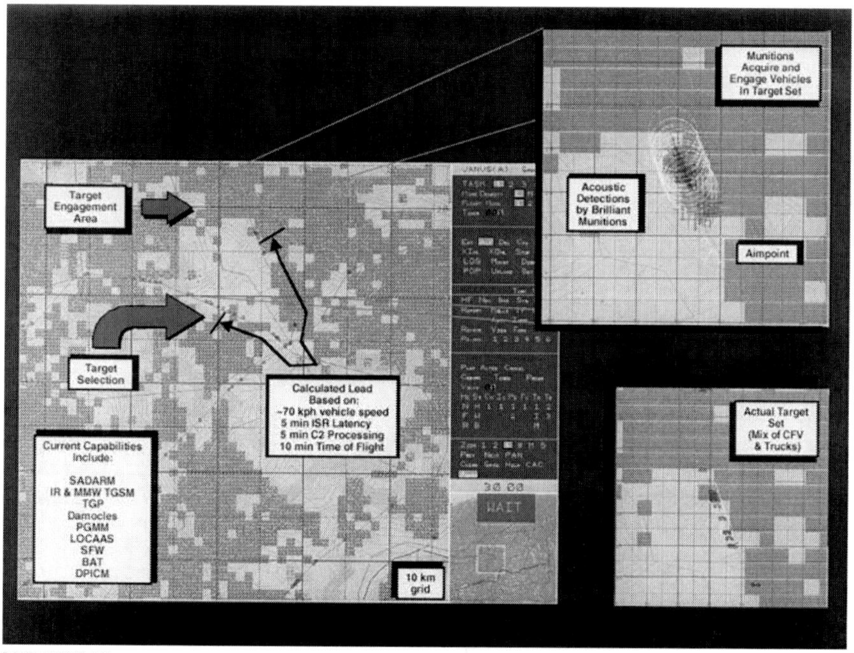

RAND *MG101-E.2*

The model provides a capability for simulating and analyzing chain logic, false-alarm rates, hulks, submunition reacquisition, shots, hits, and kills, as well as bus, munition, and submunition reliability. For example, to estimate how many vehicles are killed by a BAT, MADAM simulates the separation of the bus from the launch vehicle, the separation of submunitions from the bus, several stages of acoustic seeking and deployment by the submunitions as they descend, an IR detection stage, and a final shot/hit/kill event for each submunition. The outcome at each stage is determined, in part, by a random draw.

MADAM exists as both a standalone model and a subroutine of JANUS. Ordinarily, the standalone version is used for parametric analyses as a precursor to provide focus for force-on-force analytic runs that draw on the MADAM version that resides as a subroutine in JANUS. For this study, we used it to perform experiments in which salvos of one or two TACMS/BATs were fired at groups of Red vehicles of sizes and configurations that did not occur in the DSB '98 simulations.

Lockheed-Martin (Sunnyvale) Experience with Model Composition

The following discussion is based largely on a journal article describing the Lockheed-Martin (Sunnyvale) experience as of the late 1990s (Zeigler, Hall, and Sarjoughian, 1999) and a visit by the authors to Lockheed-Martin in August 2003 to discuss issues with Steven Hall.

Background

One of the interesting features of the Lockheed-Martin experience with composability is the fact that the company emerged in the 1990s as an agglomeration of many units, with a diversity of expertise and a treasure trove of models and simulations. However, exploiting this situation has required interfacing M&S developed by very different groups over time, using a variety of languages and platforms, and—perhaps surprisingly—often having to do so without having access to the originator's source code because the groups still have considerable separate identity and interests. Thus, the Lockheed-Martin experience has been, in a sense, a microcosm of the larger composability challenge that stimulated this monograph.

The Joint MEASURE™ (mission effectiveness analysis simulator for utility, research and evaluation) activity was designed to exploit the high-level architecture (HLA) framework and the rigorous system-specification and M&S DEVS (discrete-event simulation) methodology developed at the University of Arizona. An earlier version of the environment (Pleiades) was ported to execute on DEVS/HLA, a modern implementation of the DEVS framework that supports modeling in C++ and Java and that is compliant with the HLA.

Scope of Composition Efforts

Joint MEASURE has been used to perform analyses on advanced surface ships, underwater vehicles, and various sensor systems—underwater, terrestrial, airborne, and space-based. Table E.1 shows the scope of activities, as of the late 1990s, and the way in which components (leftmost column) were used in different combinations in the different applications (first row, except the first cell).

Discussion

The Lockheed-Martin composition activities were fundamentally motivated by the prospect of corporate benefit. They were not "science activities," but rather were practical efforts of one of America's largest defense contractors.[3] Among the hurdles the developers faced was the need for very large numbers of simulations to explore variations in system architecture and scenarios, as well as performance of various elements of a given architecture for, e.g., a space-based laser for missile defense. The model components were obtained from a variety of Lockheed-Martin groups, both geographically and organizationally distributed and with different types of expertise. Authoritative databases were also obtained from a variety of sources.

A key feature in these continuing activities has been the ability to rigorously specify and implement the component models in simulations in which reproducibility and time management are essential. The DEVS/HLA approach proved quite effective for these purposes. Furthermore, it proved very speedy, because computationally intensive applications can greatly benefit from the efficiency of discrete-event simulation methods. The concept of experimental frame is built-in and heavily exploited.

---

[3] We made no effort in the fast-track study represented by this monograph to review M&S activities comprehensively, but we wish to at least mention that a number of other ongoing activities are quite relevant. These include work at the Boeing Integration Center (BIC), a state-of-the-art facility designed for both integrative work and demonstrations of network-centric operations (see http://www.boeing.com/ids/stratarch/docs/bic_ms_a.pdf), and the Joint Distributed Engineering Plant (JDEP) and its Navy predecessor. The JDEP's effort is focused on rigorous testing of interoperability.

Table E.1
Scope of Compositions

Project Model	Critical Mobile Targets	GTS III	Arsenal Ship	Coast Guard Deep Water	Space Oper-ations Vehicle	Comm. Aero-space Vehicle	JCTS	Inte-grated System Center	Space Laser	Space Discrimin-ation	Missile Defense
Radar	X		X	X	X	X	X				X
Infrared	X	X			X		X	X	X	X	X
Missile			X				X	X	X		X
Laser								X	X	X	X
Comm.	X			X		X	X	X	X		X
C^2	X		X								X
Earth, terrain	X	X	X		X						X
Weather	X										X
Waypoint	X	X	X	X	X		X				X
Orbits	X	X			X			X	X	X	X
Ballistic trajectories			X		X	X				X	X

NOTE: Adapted from a presentation to the National Research Council study on simulation-based acquisition.

Figure E.3
Architecture of Lockheed-Martin Joint MEASURE

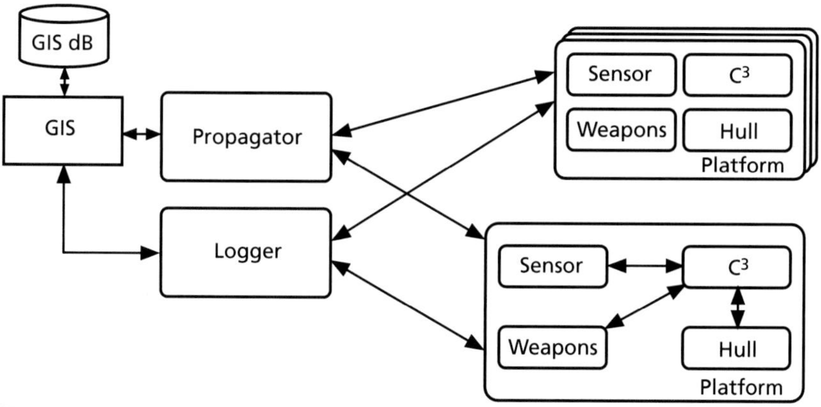

RAND *MG101-E.3*

Figure E.3 shows the architecture used, at least for the nondistributed version of Joint MEASURE. It includes a geographic information system (GIS) and its database, the simulator (indicated here by the propagator and logger), and one or more platforms to be evaluated (two, in the figure). Each platform has coupled submodels representing the hull of the platform, sensors, weapons, command and control, etc. The hull models the platform on which the sensors, weapons, and C3 capabilities exist. The logger keeps track of events. This architecture is simple, yet it has great flexibility.

Although the Lockheed-Martin activities may well represent the state of the art in complex model composability, we wish to emphasize that even with all of its elegant model specification and software tools, it is not a plug-and-play system. Anyone reading the original article will quickly appreciate that such compositions typically require a great deal of thought and some adjustments, even if software aspects of the activity go extremely well (requiring mere days to complete).

APPENDIX F

Simulation-Based Acquisition

The SBA Vision

Some composability issues are related to much-studied issues of simulation-based acquisition (SBA), an important vision toward which progress is slowly being made. We do not discuss SBA in this monograph, but it is appropriate to summarize some conclusions from past studies of the subject.

SBA is an idealized acquisition process in which all phases and programs are integrated by virtue of using a common set of databases and simulations. In the SBA context, "simulation" includes far more than the execution of dynamic models, as assumed elsewhere in this monograph. It includes, for example, high-fidelity static digital representations of key objects such as weapon systems.

Figure F.1 shows the image of SBA suggested by a 1997 study.[1] It emphasizes that success is seen as depending fundamentally on (1) a new culture, which includes model and data sharing and perpetual stakeholder involvement; (2) a new acquisition process with virtual iterative prototypes and an integrated process and product development (to include, for example, integrated product teams involved

---

[1] Report of the Industry Steering Group of DoD's Executive Committee for Modeling and Simulation (EXSIMS), Introduction, 1997. We thank Margaret Herald and Jim Coolihan for making available some of these materials. The report was described as a functional description document by the authors. See also the recent NRC study (National Research Council, 2002).

Figure F.1
Foundation Legs of Simulation-Based Acquisition

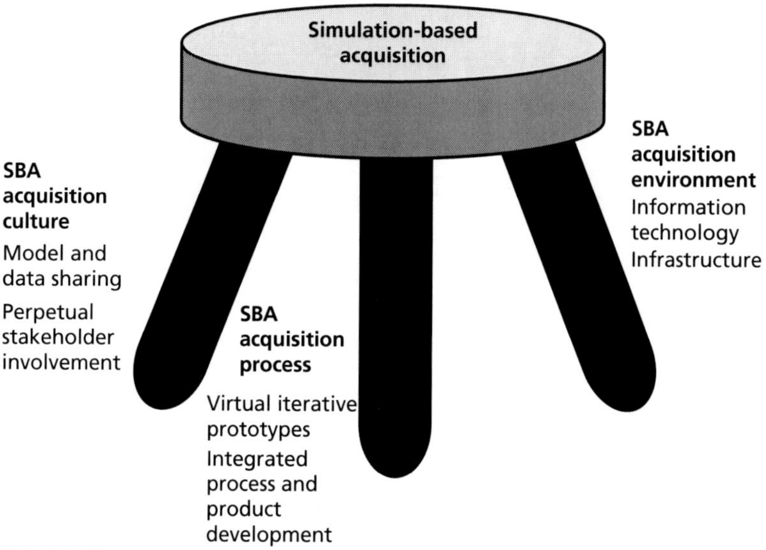

RAND *MG101-F.1*

from cradle to grave); and (3) a new acquisition environment exploiting information technology and a good infrastructure. As in the vision for composability, the hope is that SBA will lead to substantial cost savings and a speeding up of processes, while simultaneously improving product quality.

As in composability, reuse and sharing of M&S and data is a cornerstone of the vision, although most progress to date has involved static data. It is acknowledged that data reuse and sharing will require that the reliability of the data and tools be high and that the user community be educated in their use. For example, it is argued that one aspect of confidence involves reliance on the M&S tools that are used by both government and contractors. This implies reuse of standard models, simulations, and data for different systems in development. It also implies trust in a model that may have been "authenticated" by an independent organization which reviewed and approved, verified and validated, and/or certified the model and related data. Such authentication and related issues will be of paramount concern in the SBA culture. Significant efforts must be devoted to resolving such issues as the establishment of effective standards in order to gain consensus among all stakeholders. Data and configuration management are also essential to reuse, and government must invest in adequate configuration management to assure reuse.

Connection and Cautions When Relating SBA to Composability

As noted throughout this monograph, there are limits in the extent to which the goals of SBA can be achieved with many models, as distinct from pure software, purely static descriptions of objects, or simple models based on settled theory or empirical data. No one knows how far the kind of vision exemplified in the SBA documents can be driven over time, but for the near- to mid-term, it is a vision to be accepted only with extraordinary caution. It is one thing to seek an extreme degree of accuracy and commonality on something like a next-generation missile's physical characteristics and "physics" performance; it is quite another to do so when discussing, for example, the mission effectiveness of a system of doctrine, weapon systems, and command and control for long-range precision fires against furtive targets and ever-changing tactics and countermeasures, operating in close proximity to friendly forces or civilians. It should be possible to have standardized cases for the purposes of the acquisition process, but if the traditional approach of having only a few cases is used, then there should be no illusions about those cases being appropriate for the range of actual operations the systems may face. To our knowledge, the intellectual and technological groundwork has not yet been laid for creating such standard cases using the principles of capabilities-based planning.[2] That is a challenge for the near- to-mid term.

Many of the admonitions of the SBA studies carry over directly to composability. These certainly include admonitions regarding cul-

[2] For a discussion of capabilities-based planning that is mostly oriented toward force-level thinking and analysis, see Davis, 2002a.

ture problems, standards, industrial incentives, and infrastructure. We do not repeat those admonitions here, although some of the discussion in the main text is closely related.

APPENDIX G

Selected Summary Comments from a Workshop on Composability

On July 28, 2003, a workshop on composability was held at RAND's Washington, DC, office. At the end of the workshop, attendees were asked to make summary comments. Paraphrased versions of those comments are presented in Table G.1, without attribution.

Table G.1
Summary Comments from Workshop on Composability

Four concerns, reflecting a process-engineering perspective:

- *Culture.* Culture itself is an issue, since composability requires trust, and there is not a great deal of trust in the community, in part because of past abuses of the composability concept. There is need to manage expectations here.
- *Organization.* Some of the root problems are organizational, and we need some lessons-learned studies about what has and has not worked and why (e.g., for JSIMS and JWARS).
- *People.* There is need for better education and for defining a body of core knowledge to be taught.
- *Processes.* One example in the domain of processes involves data and metadata, which are currently very hard to find, to obtain access to, and to understand, even if one gets that far.

Interoperability is necessary but not sufficient for composability. MC02 illustrates this.

Composability is computationally hard. It is an NP-complete problem, although it can be dealt with.

There is need for metamodels but no consensus on what they should be like. Ideally, they would be expressed formally.

A major issue not much discussed in the workshop is the need for better data standards and better methods for describing and communicating data. Incentives are needed, but they are hard to define well, and there is clear need to make a business case if composability is to be attempted within organizations that have budget constraints.

Composability must address a real-world problem, such as a product being built.

The distinction between metamodels and metadata should be maintained.

The subject of the discussion should really be Virtual Competitions and the Representation of System Behavior, because the need is to excite industry, and industry understands the importance of good virtual competitions and how easy it is to lose a competition if the M&S isn't appropriate.

It is essential to look to the commercial markets; DoD simply doesn't have all the answers.

We need to improve the language for sharing knowledge. We need knowledge-management tools and perhaps other aids that DMSO could invest in.

Companies need tools to help evaluate systems. They do verification and validation at the lowest level, where composability issues are most tangible. Skepticism is warranted about higher-level composability.

Despite difficulties, given the right internal environment, much can be done. However, this demands a clear understanding of requirements so that a sound engineering approach can be taken, which involves documentation, iteration, mentoring, tutoring, and so on. Documentation should address the basics, such as functions, logic, control flow, and data.

More discussion is needed of how the composability issues relate to aggregation and abstraction, and of composing mechanisms versus composing phenomena. Validation of a module is different from validating a collection of modules.

Composability is in the eyes of the beholder, and a key problem is that composability is too often discussed without enough focus on the customer and his requirements. We need a solid definition of composability before we proceed, one with more meat [than is currently available] and that addresses issues such as validity for the customer's purpose. The metaphor should be not the fitting together of jigsaw-puzzle pieces, but rather having puzzle pieces with flexible edges, since adaptations will be needed. There is much to be learned from the animation industry on such things.

Documentation, including of expectations, is needed. One needs requirements.

Budget is the ultimate expression of interest. Even if we had all the components, would they be used? Would there be requisite trust? How should expectations be managed?

Tools for theory and process need to be linked. As a separate matter, we need a "business case" for composability or it won't happen.

As for semantics problems, there are perhaps eight different ways that meaning can be misconstrued which are not well understood.

More discussion of metadata and people is needed.

It seems that the time is right for revisiting the kind of discussions that occurred in 1994, before the HLA was defined. Yes, the business case is badly needed.

It is important to focus on the modeling-specific issues, rather than the more general problems of software engineering.

Composability is engineering, not art; we need good engineers.

We also need name-space management.

Distinctions should be maintained between model and simulation.

The HLA is not sufficient, and composability will go away as a notion without a revitalized vision and sponsorship. The vision should be tied to commercial developments.

Bibliography

Alberts, David S., John Garstka, Richard Hayes, and David Signori, *Understanding Information Age Warfare, CCRP*, Department of Defense, Washington, D.C, 2001.

Alberts, David S., John Garstka, and Frederick Stein, *Network Centric Warfare: Developing and Leveraging Information Technology*, CCRP Pub= lication Series, Washington, DC, 1999.

Albir, Sinan Si, *UML in a Nutshell: A Desktop Quick Reference*, Cambridge, MA: O'Reilly, 1998.

Allen, Tom, and Scott Simpkins, "Improving Defense Analysis Through Better Data Practices Workshop Summary," *Phalanx*, Vol. 36, No. 3, 2003.

Andrews, Emily B., "Establishing Standards and Specifications," in David S. Cloud, and Larry B. Rainey (eds.), *Applied Modeling and Simulation: An Integrated Approach to Development and Operations*, New York: McGraw-Hill, 1998.

Army Science Board, *Army Science Board FY 2000 Summer Study Final Report, Executive Summary*, Assistant Secretary of the Army (Acquisition, Logistics and Technology), Washington, DC, 2001.

Baldwin, Carliss Y., and Kim B. Clark, *Design Rules: The Power of Modularity*, Cambridge, MA: MIT Press, 2000.

Bigelow, James H., and Paul K. Davis, *Implications for Model Validation of Multiresolution, Multiperpective Modeling (MRMPM) and Exploratory Analysis*, Santa Monica, CA: RAND Corporation, 2003.

Brooks, Frederick P., *The Mythical Man Month: Essays on Software Engineering: Anniversary Edition*, 2d ed., New York: Addison-Wesley, 1995.

Carr, Francis H., and Lynda Myers, "Interoperability and Reuse Through a Modeling and Simulation Common Operating Environment," *Proceedings of the Software Interoperability Workshop 035-SIW-016*, Spring 2003.

Ceranowicz, Andrew, Mark Torpey, Bill Helfinstine, John Evans, and Jack Hines, "Reflections on Building the Joint Experimental Federation," *IITSEC*, 2002.

Clark, Vern, Admiral, USN, "Sea Power 21," *U.S. Navy Proceedings*, October 2002.

Cloud, David S., and Larry B. Rainey (eds.), *Applied Modeling and Simulation: An Integrative Approach to Development and Operations,* New York: McGraw-Hill, 1998.

Dahmann, Judith, and David C. Woods (eds.), "Special Issue on Distributed Interactive Simulation," *Proceedings of the IEEE*, No. 8, August 1995.

Davis, Paul K., *Representing Operational Strategies and Command-Control in the RAND Strategy Assessment System*, Santa Monica, CA: RAND Corporation, N-3232-OSD, 1990.

Davis, Paul K., *Effects-Based Operations: A Grand Challenge for the Analytical Community,* Santa Monica, CA: RAND Corporation, 2001a.

Davis, Paul K., "Adaptive Designs for Multiresolution, Multiperspective Modeling (MRMPM)," in Hessam Sarjoughian (ed.), *Discrete-Event Modeling and Simulation Technologies,* New York: Springer, 2001b.

Davis, Paul K., *Analytic Architecture for Capabilities-Based Planning, Mission-System Analysis, and Transformation,* Santa Monica, CA: RAND Corporation, 2002a.

Davis, Paul K., "Integrating Transformation Programs," Chap. 7 in Hans Binnendijk (ed.), *Transforming America's Military,* Center for National Security Policy, Washington, DC: National Defense University Press, 2002b.

Davis, Paul K., and James H. Bigelow, *Experiments in Multiresolution Modeling (MRM)*, Santa Monica, CA: RAND Corporation, 1998.

Davis, Paul K., and James H. Bigelow, *Motivated Metamodels: Synthesis of Cause-Effect Reasoning and Statistical Metamodeling*, Santa Monica, CA: RAND Corporation, 2003.

Davis, Paul K., James H. Bigelow, and Jimmie McEver, *Exploratory Analysis and a Case History of Multiresolution, Multiperspective Modeling*, Santa Monica, CA: RAND Corporation, RP-925, 2001.

Davis, Paul K., and Richard Hillestad, "Models That Cross Levels of Resolution: Issues for Design, Calibration, and Management," *Proceedings of the Winter Simulation Conference*, 1993.

Davis, Paul K., and James H. Winnefeld, *The RAND Strategy Assessment Center*, Santa Monica, CA: RAND Corporation, R-3535-NA, 1983.

Defense Modeling and Simulation Office (DMSO), "Composable Mission Space Environments," available at https://www.dmso.mil/public/warfighter/cmse (last accessed 2002).

Deitchmann, Seymour, "A Lanchester Model of Guerilla Warfare," *Operations Research,* Vol. 10, 1962, pp. 818–827.

Deitz, Paul H., Bruce Harris, Britt Bray, Jack Sheehan, Alexander Wong, and Ellen Purdy, *The Nexus of Military Missions and Means,* presented paper, 2003.

Deptula, D., Brig. Gen., USAF, "Effects-Based Operations: Change in the Nature of Warfare," available at http://www.afa.org/media/reports (last accessed 2001).

Doyle, John, "Virtual Engineering: Toward a Theory for Modeling and Simulation of Complex Systems," in National Research Council (ed.), *Modeling and Simulation, Vol. 9 in Technology for the United States Navy and Marine Corps: 2000–2035*, Washington, DC: National Academy Press, 1997, pp. 117–171.

Edmonds, Bruce, *Syntactic Measures of Complexity,* dissertation, University of Manchester, Manchester, UK, 1999.

Fishwick, Paul A., *Simulation Modeling: Design and Execution,* New York: Prentice Hall, 1995.

Fujimoto, Richard, et al., "Grand Challenges for Modeling and Simulation," available at http://www.informatik.uni-rostock.de/~lin/GC/report/index.html (last accessed 2002).

Gritton, Eugene, Paul K. Davis, Randall Steeb, and John Matsumura, *Ground Forces for a Rapidly Employable Joint Task Force,* Santa Monica, CA: RAND Corporation, 2000.

Hall, Steven B., "Advanced Simulation Center: A Report to the National Research Council's Committee on Modeling and Simulation Enhancement for 21st Century Manufacturing and Acquisition," briefing provided as a personal communication, 2000.

Harmon, S. Y., "Scientific Exploration of Simulation Phenomena," available at www.amso.army.mil/harmon (last accessed 2002).

Hofmann, Marko A., *Criteria for Decomposing Systems into Components in Modelling and Simulation—Lessons Learned with Military Simulations,* dissertation, Armed Forces University, Munich, Germany, 2003.

Holland, John H., *Hidden Order: How Adaptation Builds Complexity*, Cambridge, MA: Perseus, 1995.

Holland, John H., *Emergence: From Chaos to Order,* Cambridge, MA: Perseus, 1998.

Kapustis, Stephen, and Henry Ng, "Composable Simulations," *Proceedings of the Winter Simulation Conference,* 2002.

Law, Averill, and David W. Kelton, *Simulation Modeling and Analysis*, 2d ed., 1991.

Lehman, Meir M., "Program, Life Cycles, and Laws of Software Evolution," *Proceedings of the IEEE,* Vol. 68, No. 9, 1980.

Maier, M. W., "Architecting Principles for Systems-of-Systems," available at www.infoed.com/Open/PAPERS/systems.htm (last accessed 2002).

Matsumura, John, Randall Steeb, John Gordon, Tom Herbert, Russ Glenn, and Paul Steinberg, *Lightning over Water: Sharpening America's Capabilities for Rapid-Reaction Missions,* Santa Monica, CA: RAND Corporation, 2001.

McCabe, Thomas, "A Complexity Measure," *IEEE Transactions of Software Engineering*, Vol. SE-2, No. 4, December 1976.

Nance, Richard E., "Distributed Simulation with Federations: Expectations, Realizations, and Limitations," *Proceedings of the 1999 Winter Simulation Conference*, 1999, pp. 1026–1031.

National Academy of Sciences, *Implications of Emerging Micro and Nanotechnology*, Washington, DC: National Academy Press, 2003.

National Research Council, *Modeling and Simulation, Vol. 9 of Technology for the United States Navy and Marine Corps: 2000–2035,* Washington, D.C: National Academy Press, 1997a.

National Research Council, *Modeling and Simulation: Linking Entertainment and Defense,* Washington, DC: National Academy Press, 1997b.

National Research Council, *Ada and Beyond: Software Policies for the Department of Defense,* Washington, DC: National Academy Press, 1997c.

National Research Council, *Network Centric Naval Forces,* Naval Studies Board, Washington, DC: National Academy Press, 2000.

National Research Council, *Modeling and Simulation in Manufacturing and Defense Acquisition: Pathways to Success,* Washington, DC: National Academy Press, 2002.

Nelson, M., paper presented at annual meeting of the Military Operations Research Society, 2003.

Neyland, David L., *Virtual Combat: A Guide to Distributed Interactive Simulation*, Mechanicsburg, PA: Stackpole Books, 1997.

Owens, William A., and Edward Offney, *Lifting the Fog of War*, New York: Farrar Straus and Giroux, 2000.

Pace, Dale, "Verification, Validation, and Accreditation of Simulation Models," in Mohammad S. Obaidat and Georgios Papadimitriou (eds.), *Applied System Simulation: Methodologies and Applications*, Dordrecht, Netherlands: Kluwer Academic Publishers, 2003.

Page, Ernest H., and Jeff M. Opper, "Observations on the Complexity of Composable Simulation," *Proceedings of the 1999 Winter Simulation Conference*, 1999, pp. 553–560.

Petty, Mikel D., and Eric W. Weisel, "A Composability Lexicon," *Proceedings of the Software Interoperability Workshop*, 035-SIW-023, Spring 2003.

Pfleeger, Shari, *Software Engineering, Theory and Practice,* 2d ed., Englewood Cliffs, NJ: Prentice Hall, 2001.

Rogers, Ralph, Vince Amico, and Mark Yerkes, "The Simulation Professional Certification Program: A Status Report," *Proceedings of the 2002 Winter Simulation Conference*, Winter 2002.

Rumbaugh, James R., Stephen Blaha, Michael Blaha, William Premerlani, and Frederick Eddy, *Object-Oriented Modeling and Design*, Englewood Cliffs, NJ: Prentice Hall, 1990.

Rumsfeld, Donald, *Report of the Quadrennial Defense Review,* Department of Defense, Washington, DC, 2001.

Sage, Andrew, *Systems Management for Information Technology and Engineering,* New York: John Wiley, 1995.

Sage, Andrew P., and C. D. Cuppan, "On the Systems Engineering and Management of Systems of Systems and Federations of Systems," *Information, Knowledge, and Systems Management,* Vol. 2, No. 4, 2001, pp. 325–345.

Simon, Anthony J., "DoD Data Strategy: Transforming the Way DoD Manages Data," undated briefing, OASD(C3I) [now OASD(NII)].

Simon, Herbert, *Sciences of the Artificial*, 2d ed., Cambridge, MA: MIT Press, 1981.

Singhal, Sandeep, and Michael Zyda, *Networked Virtual Environments: Design and Implementation,* Boston, MA: Addison-Wesley, 1999.

Sisti, Alex, and Stephen Farr, "Model Abstraction Techniques: An Intuitive Overview," available at http://www.rl.af.mil/tech/papers/ModSim/ModAb_Intuitive.html.

Smith, Edward R., *Effects Based Operations: Applying Network Centric Warfare in Peace, Crisis, and War,* CCRP, Department of Defense, Washington, DC, 2003.

Speight, L. R., "Structural Variance or 'Nonmonotonicity' Effects in Combat Models: A Review," *Military Operations Research*, Vol. 8, 2003.

Starr, Stuart, "Improving Defense Analysis Through Better Data Practices: Synthesis Panel," *Report of the Synthesis Panel of a MORS Meeting on Data Practices,* 25–27 March 2003.

Szyperski, Clemens, *Component Software: Beyond Object-Oriented Programminng*, 2d ed., New York: Addison-Wesley, 2002.

Thomas, George B., *Calculus*, 10th ed., Finney, Weir, and Giordano, 2000.

Tolk, Andreas, "Avoiding Another Green Elephant—A Proposal for the Next Generation HLA Based on the Model Driven Architecture," *Proceedings of the Simulation Interoperability Workshop*, Fall 2002.

Tolk, Andreas, "A Common Framework for Military M&S and C4I Systems," *Proceedings of the Software Interoperability Conference,* Fall 2003.

Tolk, Andreas, and Michael R. Hieb, "Building and Integrating M&S Components into C4ISR Systems for Supporting Future Military Operations," *Proceedings of the Software Interoperability Workshop*, Fall 2003.

Uhrmacher, A. M., Paul A. Fishwick, and Bernard Zeigler, "Special Issue: Agents in Modeling and Simulation: Exploiting the Metaphor," *Proceedings of the IEEE*, Vol. 89, No. 2, 2001.

Uhrmacher, Adelinde, and William Swartout. "Agent-Oriented Simulation," in Mohammad S. Obaidat and Georgios Papadimitriou (eds.), *Applied System Simulation: Methodologies and Applications,* Dordrecht, Netherlands: Kluwer Academic Publishers, 2003.

U.S. Air Force Scientific Advisory Board, *Report on Information Management to Serve the Warfighter*, December 1998.

U.S. Joint Forces Command, *Millennium Challenge 2002 Modeling and Simulation Federation,* Norfolk, VA: Joint Forces Command, 2002.

"Vectors: A History of Vectors," available at http://occawlonline.pearsoned.com/bookbind/pubbooks/thomas_awl/chapter1/medialib/custom3/topics/vectors.htm.

Weisel, Eric W., Mikel D. Petty, and Roland R. Mielke, "Validity of Models and Classes of Models in Semantic Composability," *Proceedings of the Software Interoperability Conference*, 03F-SIW-073, Fall 2003.

Zeigler, Bernard, "Towards a Systems Methodology for Object-Oriented Software Analysis," Chap. 6 of a forthcoming book, 2003.

Zeigler, Bernard, Steven B. Hall, and Hessam S. Sarjoughian, "Exploiting HLA and DEVS to Promote Interoperability and Reuse in Lockheed's Corporate Environment," *Simulation*, Vol. 73, No. 5, 1999, pp. 288–295.

Zeigler, Bernard P., Herbert Praehofer, and Tag Gon Kim, *Theory of Modeling and Simulation*, 2d ed., *Integrating Discrete Event and Continuous Complex Systems,* San Diego, CA: John Wiley, 2000.

Zeigler, B., and H. Sarjoughian, "Implications of M&S Foundations for the V&V of Large Scale Complex Simulation Models," presented paper, available at http://www.acims.arizona.edu/EVENTS/MSV&V_ACIMS.pdf (last accessed 2002).